just friends
// guarding your heart for a wonderful someday

mike ray //
cary schmidt

Copyright © 2009 by Striving Together Publications.
All Scripture quotations are taken from the
King James Version.

First published in 2009 by Striving Together
Publications, a ministry of Lancaster Baptist Church,
Lancaster, CA 93535. Striving Together Publications
is committed to providing tried, trusted, and proven
books that will further equip local churches to carry
out the Great Commission. Your comments and
suggestions are valued.

All rights reserved. No part of this book may be
reproduced, stored in a retrieval system, or transmitted
in any form or by any means—electronic, mechanical,
photocopy, recording, or otherwise—without written
permission of the publisher, except for brief
quotations in printed reviews.

Striving Together Publications
4020 E. Lancaster Blvd.
Lancaster, CA 93535
800.201.7748

Edited by Amanda Michael, Sarah Michael,
and Danielle Mordh
Cover design by Andrew Jones
Layout by Craig Parker
Special thanks to our proofreaders.

ISBN 978-1-59894-072-5
Printed in the United States of America

Dedication

Mike Ray
To my teenagers

My prayer is that you will be pure, in the center of God's will, and very happy and successful in your marriages. May this book aid in reaching those goals.

Cary Schmidt
To my children—Lance, Larry, and Haylee

You guys are AWESOME! May God guard your incredible hearts so that you can experience the wonderful someday that Mom and I have together! We love you with all of our hearts!

Contents

Acknowledgments vii
A Word from the Authors xi
Introduction xv

PART ONE—See the Big Picture
1. Mutations, Confusion, and Transition 3
2. A Biblical View of Guy/Girl Relationships 17
3. A Closer Look at Biblical Friendships 25
4. Erasing Hollywood's Model 35
5. Discovering God's Model 45
6. A Wonderful "Someday!" 55

PART TWO—Make Big Choices
7. Choose "The Right Person at the Right Time" . .69
8. Choose God's Will 77
9. Choose Controlled Emotions—Part 1 91
10. Choose Controlled Emotions—Part 2 97
11. Choose Purity—Part 1 109
12. Choose Purity—Part 2 117
13. Choose "No Touch"—Part 1 131
14. Choose "No Touch"—Part 2 139
15. Choose Family First 149
16. Choose True Love 159
17. Choose "Just Friends" 165

PART THREE—Get the Details Right
18. Becoming the Right Person 177
19. Setting the Right Pace 187
20. Advantages of "Just Friends" 197
21. Treating People Right 203
22. Dress for Success 213
23. When You Can't Act Normal 223

Conclusion 229
Just Friends in Review 233

Acknowledgments

From Mike Ray

Working with young people in ministry for the last forty years, I have found this is one topic I teach on that always secures the attention—boy meets girl. I constantly run into married couples who are teaching my earlier material to their children, who read it themselves as young adults. Wow! That really makes me feel old!

I am very thankful to Cary Schmidt for taking my original thoughts, adding his own writings and developing a more relevant format for today's Christian young people. Every young adult, student worker, and every parent should visit this book often. *Just Friends* is priceless. May it be a refreshing pause on the journey to your marriage altar.

Special Thanks to…

My beautiful wife for being faithful to me these last twenty-nine plus years. You are my college sweetheart.

My daughters, Charity and Faith, for practicing all the things in this book and being examples to your siblings and teen group.

My sons-in-law, Eric Marczak and Ely Reynolds, for being so good to my daughters. You are great sons-in-law, and God is using you in a mighty way in ministry.

My sons, Jonathan, Paul and Stephen, who have been such a blast to spend time with. Thank you for making Mom and Dad so proud by your attitudes and involvement in ministry. May this book aid in your journey toward marriage.

My teenagers in our teen group in Napa, California. You are the first generation Christians. May you take the treasures in these pages and make them yours—show everyone in California how to do it right.

The parents in our church. Thank you for letting me serve right alongside of you. God bless you as we reach the rest of our kids side by side.

Brother Cary Schmidt for practicing these principles as a teenager and being able to say to teens across America, "Do as I did *and* as I say."

The Striving Together Publications staff for helping make this project a reality. You are such a blessing.

Last, and certainly not least, my Saviour, Jesus Christ, for saving me and guiding me through the teen years and for graciously giving me a great marriage, great

Acknowledgments

children, wonderful church and ministry and friends of a lifetime.

From Cary Schmidt

I thank the Lord Jesus for allowing me to serve Him! His faithfulness is amazing and His mercies unspeakable!

I also thank my amazing wife, Dana! She is my "wonderful someday!" A book can be a consuming project, but she faithfully loves me and encourages me with each one. She is my best friend and an amazing life companion!

I thank Pastor Paul Chappell for loving my family, allowing us to serve at Lancaster Baptist, and for allowing me to help with Striving Together Publications. It's a great privilege to be on his team and to call him Pastor!

I thank the Lancaster Baptist Church and West Coast Baptist College students and families. It is a great joy to serve the Lord in your midst and to watch Him work in your lives.

I thank the incredible people I work with who have the unfortunate responsibility to read the first drafts of what I write. They lovingly and skillfully make books like this far better. Thank you to Amanda Michael, Sarah Michael, and Danielle Mordh for reading and making so many early, positive contributions. Thank you to my sons Lance and Larry, and Hillarie Shannon for reading the first draft as well—your insight was very helpful. Thank you to our proofreaders who spent many hours studying every detail of this manuscript. Their volunteer efforts are invaluable, and I am deeply grateful for their help!

I thank Craig Parker for his help and skill on layout and Andrew Jones for his wonderful cover design!

Finally, thank you to Pastor Mike Ray! What a great honor it is to work with him on this project. Pastor Ray impacted me and my wife greatly when we were teenagers, and he has always been a profound encourager and godly influence to us since that time.

A Word from the Authors

Hey! Read this! It's from our hearts.

Thanks for picking up *Just Friends*. You're about to embark on a wonderful, growing journey of learning about young adult emotions and relationships. There is much to learn, but first we want you to know where this book is coming from and who it's for. It's coming from the hearts of two fairly regular guys. We are:

Two grown-up teenagers. We remember very clearly what it was like to feel how you feel.

Two pastors. We've spent a lot of time with people your age for a lot of years! In fact we're starting to get sick of you. (That was a joke.)

Two student counselors. We've spent thousands of hours talking and counseling with young adults in high school and college about the issues addressed in this book.

Two marriage and family counselors. We've counseled many marriages, pre-marriages, and families. We love helping people have strong relationships.

Two very happily married guys! We've both been married a pretty long time—Mike Ray much longer, because he's a grandfather!

Two fathers. We've had a great time raising our own kids. Cary Schmidt's kids are still teens, and Mike Ray's kids are young adults starting families of their own. We know the inside track of family and young adult life.

Two happy guys. We both really love life and enjoy living it! We love serving God and love to laugh. We believe God can help you build a happy future as well.

Two guys who care about you. Your world would love to chew you up, spit you out, and grind you into the dirt. We have poured our hearts out in this book to help you survive.

This book has three parts. Part one is about God's big picture. Part two is about making big choices. And part three is about the practical side of healthy friendships. This book is one of two books. This one is directed at young adults in teen and college years. If you are a teenager, these principles will help you avoid some common teen pitfalls. If you are a post-high school young adult, most of this book is quite applicable to you, with the exception that you have come through the transitions mentioned in chapter one—and you will

A Word from the Authors

wish you had known some of these things sooner. Either way, these truths will help you establish your heart upon God's purposes.

Every few chapters you will find an assignment for practical application. As you read, be sure to work through these studies to apply what you have learned.

The second book, soon to follow, will be directed at post-high school young adults—those eighteen and above—and will focus primarily on taking the *right relationship* from friendship to marriage at the *right time* and the *right way*.

We invite you, for the rest of this book, to open your heart and consider God's principles as they apply to your guy/girl relationships and friendships. Your entire future depends upon how seriously you take God's principles and how you respond to the truth presented in these pages.

We pray you will enjoy this book, but even more so, we pray that it will change your life and preserve your future!

Thanks for reading!

Sincerely,

Cary Schmidt and Mike Ray

Introduction

Keep thy heart with all diligence; for out of it are the issues of life.
—PROVERBS 4:23

So what is this thing between guys and girls? Do we call it *dating*? *Attraction*? *Interest*? Do we formalize the process and call it *courtship*, *romance*, or how about that really great Bible word—*espousal*? (Yikes! It's definitely too soon for that!)

Do we call it being in love, being in like, or how about being insane?! (That last one sounds like many young adult relationships we've seen.) We could go a little less cool and call it going steady, going together, or even going crazy!

We could call it going out, going around, seeing someone, liking someone, owning someone, controlling someone, or how about being absolutely obsessed over someone? Flipped? Cloud nine? Starry-eyed? La-la land?

Ah—how about *infatuation*! No, that's too surface sounding. *Love*? Nope, that's too "lifetime commitment-ish." Puppy love? Too childish. Teen romance? Oh brother! That sounds like some gushy magazine title! Head-in-the-clouds? Heartthrob?

Let's just go with Bambi and call it *twitterpated*!

Okay. We give up! We all know there's something between guys and girls, and we all know it starts when you become a teenager. But no one really knows what to call it, and for some strange reason *everyone* is afraid to talk about it—especially parents! So, what do you call it? Hmmm...

Well, let's go with your term. In fact, let's go with tens of thousands of young people who have come before you. There is a term coined deep in the ancient recesses of youth history—probably sometime before Moses' teen years—a term that every teenager since that time has used to define this thing between guys and girls. A term that has universal meaning to all thirteen to nineteen year-olds—and beyond! To you and your "friend" it most likely means, "We like each other!" But to everyone else, it means, "Back off! We are embarrassed about this!"

The term? *Just friends*!

Most likely you've said it. Most likely someone has said it to you! "We're *just friends*!" Sometimes you mean

Introduction

it, sometimes you mean something a little stronger, but a bit harder to define. You know what I'm talking about. Guys just like girls. And girls just like guys. And there's something in all of us that actually "likes being liked"! And woe to the heart that feels "unlikable" in this cruel world of *just friends*.

Whether you're for it, against it, afraid of it, confused by it, or dazzled by it—it's here, and it's for real. We're not even saying we condone all these words or "types of attraction." We're just saying they exist, and it's time to understand a reasonable and biblical approach to them.

So, whatever you call it, we want to first say, "Congratulations! You are normal." Being attracted to the opposite gender is neither wrong nor abnormal. In fact, it's a great, wonderful, God-given gift! But it's also a large new world of powerful emotions and confusing feelings that can actually be dangerous and hurtful to young hearts.

The sad thing is, many young adults are left to themselves in this area. We don't talk enough with our parents about these matters. On top of this, our culture is hammering you constantly with twisted distortions of what true love and lifetime romance is really all about. In our sex-crazed climate, you can't buy a loaf of bread or walk through a mall without being constantly slam-dunked with lies and deceptive imagery about love and relationships.

If there is one thing that you should learn from our world's twisted version of love and sex-craziness, it's that they are *not happy* and their way obviously *doesn't work*! They can't even stay married much less find true love and intimacy with one person. They are like starving refugees scavenging for any scrap of love or pleasure they can scrounge up! What a miserable way to live!

In this book, we would like to introduce to you a much better way. The fact is, God desires to give you a full heart, a full life, and all the love you could ever need. But it all starts with Him and happens according to His principles and His timetable. The danger comes *while* you are growing in His principles and *waiting* on His timetable. The devil would love for you to "jump the gun"! He wants you to do permanent damage to your heart and life before you ever arrive at the lifetime love that God designed.

Consider this question. Do you value your heart? Do you value the stability, the spiritual strength, and the emotional wellness of your life? If so, then this book will help you protect your heart as you journey through some very dangerous minefields of emotions and early attraction.

God says in Proverbs 4:23, "Keep thy heart with all diligence; for out of it are the issues of life." As a young person, you are in the middle of the most important years of your life—the years your values and character are established and the years when you are *becoming* the person God wants you to be. These are the years when you are preparing for a lifetime mate and a lifetime calling.

Introduction

To survive the lies of culture and to someday experience the unbelievable blessings of God in your life, you must decide to guard and protect your heart—to base all of your friendships and youthful attractions upon the Bible. Are your philosophies of guy/girl friendships based upon the world's warped ideas and lies or upon God's truth?

The purpose of this book is to give you a biblical foundation upon which to establish your heart—to give you truth in a world of lies. We want you to have a greater understanding of how to deal with attraction toward the opposite gender without letting those attractions eat you alive! Many young adults are really messing up their lives. You don't have to be one of them.

So, regardless of what we call this thing between guys and girls, it's actually pretty great! It was God's idea to begin with. And if you go with His plan, you're going to love where He leads you.

So, read on. Here's what to do if you are *twitterpated*!

PART ONE
See the Big Picture

*To understand young adult
relationships, we must understand
God's view. We must see His perspective.
He always has the big picture in mind.*

ONE

Mutations, Confusion, and Transition
a biblical view of your youth

"Who rode their bicycle through your mouth?!" It was during my seventh grade year, and those were the first rather hurtful words I (Cary) heard at Wednesday night Bible study when I arrived at church with my new "headgear"! As if braces and a retainer weren't enough torture, my orthodontist had to wire an erector set to my jaw! And even worse, he then made me wear it—IN PUBLIC! What a devastating thing it is to walk around with a hamster-sized Ferris wheel strapped to your face!

Then I remember the day I was asked if I was wearing "water skis for tennis shoes." I was thirteen and my feet had grown faster than the rest of my body, giving me that really cool "Ronald McDonald look." If I had painted them red, people would have been asking me for autographs! Then there was the "shrimp factor"! In junior high I was really rinky-dink sized. I was all of five feet two inches, while every girl in my class was nearing six feet! I was the smallest guy in the youth group. My legs were so skinny that people called me "chicken-legs," and I weighed ninety pounds dripping wet and bench pressed the same! *Identity crisis* doesn't even begin to describe it. I didn't think I would make it through those terrible times.

> It's pretty tough just being a young adult, much less navigating the overwhelming emotions of attraction.

The point is—it's pretty tough just being a young adult, much less navigating the overwhelming emotions of *attraction*. Your teen years are a time of radical change and transformation in several major areas. So, before we try to dig into the nuts and bolts of guy/girl relationships, let's explore just what you're up against during these years.

Understanding Physical Changes

The first area of dramatic change during the teen years is *physical change*! Have you noticed how much you are changing day-by-day and month-by-month? More importantly, have you considered the impact of those changes in all of life? If you are fifteen or older, go grab

One—Mutations, Confusion, and Transition

a picture of yourself from two years ago and compare. *A lot* has changed! Guys never change more quickly and radically than they do between ages fourteen and seventeen. For girls it happens a year or so sooner—which accounts for girls sometimes being taller and interested in older guys. It also accounts for their favorite insult to the guys their age—*"you are so immature!"*

Sometimes we fail to understand these changes (that often seem more like mutations) and to consider how they impact our existence. Teens grow fast, that's a given. But have you considered the physical energy that is consumed to produce that growth? Have you considered the emotional impact of such physical drain? Have you connected the dots on the awkwardness, fatigue, hunger, and insecurity that accompany this radical mutation happening in you?

No wonder you eat so much, sleep so much, and seem to fumble around physically at times. No wonder you worry about what your friends think of you—you can barely keep up with the change yourself! Let's break it down. What are you dealing with because of this fast physical growth?

1. Awkward coordination. Most young people go through at least a year or two of awkward coordination with their growing feet and figure. What feels like clumsiness might simply be a fast-growing body and a mind and reflexes still trying to catch up!

2. Clothing doesn't fit right. Clothing or shoes that fit well last week suddenly feel tight or cramped.

What you thought you liked two weeks ago now feels awkward or goofy. This goes beyond petty, style-conscious insecurities. The reality is, when you're a teenager, clothing and shoes you bought three days ago sometimes just don't fit for long.

3. Physical features stand out. Teens generally walk around all day feeling "weird." Admit it. You often have the feeling like you stand out, stick out, or don't "fit in." The good news is, the feeling doesn't represent reality. You fit in quite well with everybody else your age, because every teen is dealing with these same changes and awkward transitions. So relax. You might feel like a mutant, but you live in a world of mutants. You're going to make it.

4. Personal hygiene becomes an issue. Teenagers are ruthless on each other when it comes to smells and hygiene habits. During these years your body goes through several internal and external changes that make it require better upkeep. Showering more often (at least daily), wearing deodorant, shaving, and making time in your morning for basic hygiene routines is now essential—unless you just enjoy being ridiculed by others!

5. Sensitivity to appearance. Have you ever had a bad hair day? A bad pimple day? Do you wake up every morning not liking the way you look? This is one of the most frustrating parts of "teen-ness." At your age, you just care a lot more about how you look—and combined

One—Mutations, Confusion, and Transition

with all the changes you're dealing with, that can be a real killer on your morning attitude!

6. Adult sexual desires become real. This is the time when young minds occupy adult-ish bodies and you don't yet understand, value, or know how to manage these new desires. That's what this book is about. All of culture is working against you to enlarge, distort, and pervert those desires. But God will help you *protect* them and *direct* them into a life-long relationship with the *right person* at the *right time*.

What do all these physical changes mean? Well, first it means you need to be patient. You are growing and you will get through this time. Second, it means you need to be balanced. Teenagers need about ten hours of sleep each night! That's not a preference; it's a medical fact. The amount of change taking place in your body requires a good night's rest. Without it, you're going to be a lot more irritable, confused, and frustrated. You'll be a monster to live with. You'll be surprised how often a rebellious or antagonistic spirit in your heart can change with a good, long night's sleep. So give everybody else a break and get some rest.

Physical changes are real and they are massive! They impact your spirit, your heart, and your whole world. But that's just the first area of change. Let's move on.

Understanding Mental and Intellectual Change

Have you ever heard of your *frontal lobe*? It's what helps you have reason and judgment—to be able to weigh consequences and control impulses. In other words, it's what keeps you from cliff diving and overdosing on chocolate cake.

Well, it is a medical fact that your frontal lobe is only now developing, which means you tend to rely upon emotions and give in to impulses much more quickly. This is really bad news when it comes to guy/girl attractions. And this is also why many young people tend to take serious risks with no thought of the consequences—like driving fast or engaging in extreme sports stunts.

What does this mean? It means, until your frontal lobe is out of the oven, you need help making decisions. There's nothing wrong with this and no need to pretend your frontal lobe is complete. Just accept the facts and trust the people God has given you to guide your life. For all practical purposes, your parents, your pastor, and other godly authorities *are* your frontal lobe until yours is done! No wonder the devil tries to get you to rebel against these people. He would rather have you functioning without a frontal lobe. You're much more vulnerable to his traps when your brain is unwired.

1. Brain under construction—thinking skills temporarily out of service. The Boston Globe reported

One—Mutations, Confusion, and Transition

on November 10, 2005, "Teenagers' brains aren't getting bigger as they grow: The brain cells, called neurons, are simply rearranging, making new connections, and pruning unnecessary ones to speed and reroute the flow of thought." Other studies have recently reported that *every single brain cell* is literally recreated and rewired between the ages of twelve and twenty! Think about that for a moment. What an astounding statistic!

All these years we've made such a big deal about losing baby teeth and growing adult ones—even to the point of getting money from the *Tooth Fairy*! If a kid can collect a couple bucks for losing a tooth, how should we celebrate *growing a new brain*?! I think we should campaign for the establishment of a "Brain Fairy"! Only, instead of giving out cash, she could give cars, computers, and college scholarships.

All this to say, not only is your frontal lobe forming, your whole brain is rewiring itself right now. It is a medical, scientific fact that you are undergoing radical mental reconstruction. This should make you more dependent upon the Lord and godly authorities as you grow into adulthood. There's nothing wrong with trusting adults (whose brains are whole) while your brain adds a room and remodels its other floors!

2. The biblical connection that medicine doesn't make. Long before these medical studies were released, God's Word commanded us to engage in spiritual growth during these years. Deuteronomy 6:7–9 teaches, "And thou shalt teach them diligently unto thy children, and shalt talk of them when thou sittest in thine house, and when thou walkest by the way, and when thou liest down, and when thou risest up. And thou shalt bind them for a sign upon thine hand, and they shall be as frontlets between thine eyes. And thou shalt write them upon the posts of thy house, and on thy gates." Proverbs 22:6 teaches, "Train up a child in the way he should go: and when he is old, he will not depart from it."

Do you realize the gift that God has given to you right now? What better time to ingrain a brain with biblical principles and godly wisdom than when it is still being wired? It's like installing new software for the first time on a fresh hard drive. Truly, these years are formational and foundational for your future. They are the best years to grow in God's grace with a fresh set of brain cells! Again, no wonder the devil tries to fill your mind with trash through music and entertainment. No wonder he wants you to tune out the teaching of God's Word with grunge music. He's trying to corrupt that new brain. Don't let him have the pleasure!

Understanding Emotional Changes

There's one more major area of change. First let's discuss the symptoms. Do you ever experience any radical or sudden mood changes? You know—one moment everything's fine, the next you feel like the world is falling

One—Mutations, Confusion, and Transition

apart. Do you go from momentary happiness to instant frustration? Maybe you've even surprised yourself with some sudden outburst or anger? Have you noticed that one day you can feel like you're on top of the world, and the next day you feel depressed and want to completely withdraw from society and live under a rock?

Young adults experience a wide variety of *emotional changes*. Your world has suddenly become a lot more random and unpredictable than it has ever been, and this can make you feel rather impulsive, compulsive, and even *insane* at times. But then again, I know some adults who would fit nicely into those categories, so let's cut you some slack.

Consider the factors that contribute to your emotional world. We've already talked about a body that is growing and easily exhausted. We've seen a brain remodeling itself. More pressure at school, more responsibilities in life, a busier schedule, less sleep and less family time also contribute to an emotional world under extreme pressure. Sometimes you would like to just go to your room and cry, and you might not even know why.

On top of this, many young people have faced extremely difficult situations like abuse, broken homes, and painful loss. This puts the emotional stress over the top. Let's talk some more about it. Here are the things that radically impact your emotional world.

1. Changing relationships. Every relationship in your world changes during your teenage years. Adults expect more from you at home and at school. Your parents are probably going through life changes too—including financial pressures and other things that you might not be aware of—which would make them more easily frustrated at you. Everybody starts expecting you to be an adult, even yourself, and yet, it's all very new and you know you're in over your head.

2. Desperate for acceptance and identity. More than ever, your life is filled with insecurity and a need for acceptance. Many young adults grope for an identity through clothing styles, pop-culture, and a boyfriend or girlfriend. You might call it "being cool." What you really mean is "being accepted." We just can't handle it if we don't "fit in." There's not an alternative for "not fitting in." If we don't fit in, we must fix it, or at least that's how we feel.

Often people your age seek emotional stability in relationships and friendships outside the home, which can lead to bad decisions. *God desires to be your stability,* and He desires to give you friendships and influences that strengthen you toward Him, not pull you away. We'll see this more in the next chapter.

3. Romantic attractions increase. Part physical and part emotional—you just start liking the opposite gender. This life-change is made worse by the assault of a culture and information-age obsessed with sex and perversion. This is a wonderful part of being a young adult if these emotions are handled God's way. But all

One—Mutations, Confusion, and Transition

of Satan's darts are aimed at you, and to survive you're going to have to walk very wisely.

4. Fears of the future. Many are scared of what lies ahead. You long for stability, and your new "young-adult world" seems much less stable than your elementary years. More and more, young adults are choosing not to "grow up" even into their twenties and thirties. Some people your age see adults messing up their lives and reason, "Why would I want that?" Many have witnessed firsthand the misery of failed marriages and broken homes, and fear growing up and doing the same. Most people your age don't know how to chart the right course.

Take a moment and think about these emotional factors! These are BIG! And at any moment, when one of these comes crashing down on your heart, you're going to feel pretty cruddy. Even writing this makes our emotions unpredictable! We're going to take a break and cry for a while.

So what do we do? How do we navigate this emotional blasting zone called "teen years"? Well, let's wrap up this chapter with a few thoughts.

First, it's no wonder a guy/girl relationship *seems* so great! In error we could think—what better way to help me deal with this time than to have a *special someone* who makes me feel accepted, likeable, loved, and cared about—no matter how huge that zit on my face is?! On the surface it seems like a great solution.

Second, this is a *really bad time* to get into a serious guy/girl relationship. I'm talking about the kind that is exclusive—just the two of us—the kind that becomes syrupy, romantic, consuming, and emotionally overwhelming. New emotions, a developing brain, frustrating changes—these all make for a relatively unstable world. Why would you want to make it even more unstable by adding your own personal soap opera?

Too often young relationships become too much, too soon—a sort of pretend love that makes you feel better only briefly. These usually only lead to more hurt and confusion. It's better, for now, to avoid this emotional trap. It usually leads to a lot of pain, and you already have a full plate of life-transitions to deal with.

So, if the immediate solution isn't to go find a boyfriend or girlfriend, what is the right response to these changes? Here are a few suggestions:

1. Spend time with God. Ultimately, all spiritual stability comes from building your life on the Rock! The only way you will ever have emotional and spiritual stability is as you develop a personal relationship with your awesome Heavenly Father. As you learn to cast "all your care upon him," (1 Peter 5:7) He truly will establish your heart with grace (2 Thessalonians 3:3, Hebrews 13:9).

For instance, when was the last time you told God exactly how you feel and what you're going through (if ever)? There's nothing that can replace being alone with

One—Mutations, Confusion, and Transition

God, opening His Word, and letting Him speak to your heart. You must begin walking with God now and never stop. Nothing will give you a more settled heart, more stable emotions, and a more secure identity than time with Him!

2. Time with family. You need time with your parents and godly authorities. If you will survive these years, they must be your best friends and closest companions. Every moment you spend developing a strong relationship with Mom or Dad is a moment that God will settle your heart. Open up to your parents; make it a priority to spend time with them; and listen to their advice. If they are busy, then ask them for more time. If you don't have parents, then go to the next-in-line authority figure—maybe a grandparent, a relative, a teacher, or a youth pastor. You don't have a lot of time left with these people, so make it count while you can.

> Nothing will give you a more settled heart, more stable emotions, and a more secure identity than time with God!

3. Comic relief. God says that "a merry heart doeth good like a medicine" (Proverbs 17:22)! Young adults love to laugh, and that's on purpose. That's one of God's greatest gifts to you. Over the years, we have seen young people laugh at the most unusual times, and it is then that we have learned that laughter is God's way of helping you cope with the burdens of growing up!

Laughter at the right things at the right time does something wonderful and spiritual to align your emotions with God's stabilizing grace. Now, honestly, the world is producing the kind of comedy that is undeniably and extremely displeasing to God. This is NOT the kind of laughter we are referencing.

Learn to laugh at yourself. Learn to laugh with your family. Learn to see the light side of being a young adult, and be sure to get a good laugh out of it every now and then. God has a great sense of humor—after all, He is the one who created laughter! Laughter at the right things will just keep your heart and perspective balanced and sane.

So the summary of all of this is simple: *you feel like a freak because you are one.*

Okay, that was a joke. Why aren't you laughing?

Seriously, the good news is, you will survive this! You will get through it. It is important for you to understand that these *physical*, *mental*, and *emotional* changes are normal and that they will end one day. Accept them as God's way of slowly turning you into an adult—and decide to seek His help daily. Now that we understand that the teen years are a disaster waiting to happen, let's take a look at how guy/girl friendships impact the situation.

A Biblical View of Guy/Girl Relationships

The great thing about the Bible is that it has the answers for every situation of life! The Bible is *God's thoughts to man*—it is His perspective and His ways defined and described so we can live our lives accordingly. And when it comes to young attractions and friendships, God has plenty to say.

Since *dating* is never really mentioned in the Bible and *friendship* is, and since young adults usually prefer to say, "we're just friends"—we're going to go with that. God gives attraction, and God gives great friendships. And we believe that well-restrained attraction between godly friends can truly help you and prepare you for God's call on your life.

When you step back and take all of God's instruction about love and relationships, a few things become very clear. For young people, it's more about establishing healthy friendships than it is about falling in love. It's more about growing close to God and walking with Him than it is about growing close to a boyfriend or girlfriend. It's more about preparing for a lifetime love than it is about finding a temporary one.

Your life, somewhere in the future, is most likely headed towards marriage. While this isn't God's will for everybody, it is His will for most. With that in mind, every friendship, every relationship, and every attraction should take on a big-picture perspective. You will most likely one day give your whole life to another person as a spouse. And while it may seem far off, right now you are preparing for that day. You are becoming the person your spouse will marry.

Because of this, one of the first things we urge you to do is to view all of your young adult attractions and friendships through this thought—*I am preparing for God's will!* Keep the big picture in mind. God is maturing you and keeping you for someone or something special, and you don't want to mess up that future before it even begins!

Therefore, it makes sense that your young adult years should be more focused on godly friendships than on pretend romance. If you're not ready to get married, why act like you're married—especially with someone who will most likely be *someone else's* spouse? It's much wiser to focus on keeping God first and on developing godly friendships that will prepare you for what is to come.

Principles of Guy/Girl Friendships

Here are some principles that God shares relating to attraction, love, and eventually marriage:

1. Godly friendship is a good thing. Proverbs 17:17 teaches, "A friend loveth at all times, and a brother is born for adversity." It is a good thing when Christian girls and guys can be together in ways that honor the Lord and sharpen their lives for God's glory. Good friendships do much to prepare you spiritually, socially, and relationally for a wonderful future.

2. Guy/girl attraction is a natural thing. Genesis 2:18 says, "And the LORD God said, It is not good that the man should be alone; I will make him an help meet for him." A strange thing happens to a boy at age twelve or thirteen. Mom doesn't have to remind him to take a bath anymore. His hair is usually combed. He gives up his membership to the "girl-hater's" club down the street. (One second grade boy claimed he had nineteen girlfriends. He started early.) Girls soon put their dolls in storage and start noticing boys and telephones a little more.

During our youth, God puts in each of us a natural desire to spend more time with the opposite gender. In early childhood, we spend most of our time with parents. But as we get older, we spend more of our time with our own gender. After that, our time becomes a bit more divided between guys and girls. Finally during later teens and college years, even more time is spent with the opposite gender until eventually it's time to choose a spouse.

3. Guy/girl friendship should be Bible-based. If you really want to know how to conduct yourself in friendship, you can find the answers in the Scriptures. Study the lives of people in the Bible in respect to their marriages, morality, and standards. A wise Christian will bathe himself in the book of Proverbs daily. The Bible ought to be the center of a godly friendship. It is the relationship manual for mature Christian young people. It will keep you clean (Psalm 119:9) and in the center of God's will (Romans 12:1–2).

4. Godly friendship is about fellowship. First John 1:3 says, "That which we have seen and heard declare we unto you, that ye also may have fellowship with us: and truly our fellowship is with the Father, and with his Son Jesus Christ." Philippians 1:4–5 says, "Always in every prayer of mine for you all making request with joy, For your fellowship in the gospel from the first day until now." Acts 2:42 says, "And they continued stedfastly in the apostles' doctrine and fellowship, and in breaking of bread, and in prayers."

God's philosophy of friendship is about fellowship! It is about the bond of love and connection that God puts in the hearts of His children. There is unity—a

Two—A Biblical View of Guy/Girl Relationships

togetherness among God's people because we belong to Christ. And that unity should cause us to strengthen each other. Simply put, you should be a better Christian because of your friendships.

In the book of Acts, Christians ate together, went soulwinning together, prayed together, and served together. Even so, your friendships should be Christ-focused and others-focused.

Many young people don't understand true friendship. Their friendships are more like *mutual insecurity dependencies*—"me-focused." They are two very insecure people overly depending on each other to meet their emotional needs. The same is true for many so-called "dating relationships"—they are more about "needing to be liked" than about becoming like Christ.

> You should be a better Christian because of your friendships.

Mature Christians have a different perspective. They find their acceptance and love in Christ, and then their friendships are focused more on fellowshipping and serving.

We encourage you to bring your young adult friendships into this thinking—*fellowship*! If you are already a friend to the other young adults in your church or youth group, you will most likely find someone you're attracted to sooner or later. This doesn't mean you should start acting like a dysfunctional mental case. While you might get nervous and feel a bit awkward, in reality, you should just enjoy the friendship and develop it through godly fellowship. After all, God says that He wants us to have fellowship.

Too many young people get weird when they "like" someone. The weirdness is a product of not knowing what to do with these interesting new feelings. When that "special person" is near, your heart speeds up, your palms get sweaty, your brain gets confused, and a thousand thoughts and emotions start flooding your mind. If you don't carefully respond, you'll start doing what feels "natural"—which usually leads to being physical and being exclusive—separated from the group and wallowing in your own private soap opera. Not only is that NOT fun, it's dangerous. Godly friendships don't progress this way. We'll talk about this more later.

> The road that leads to marriage begins with real, authentic, godly friendships.

When youthful couples always want to be isolated away from the group and alone, it's never a good sign. This tends to be a "non-Christian" type of friendship. Your goal as a Christian in your friendship ought to be to help that person grow in the Lord and be the best Christian he or she can be for God. God has made you spiritual brothers and sisters and wants you to be concerned about one another's spiritual well-being.

Decide now that you will learn from the person you are attracted to and that you will help them learn from you. See their weaknesses and their strengths, and try to

Two—A Biblical View of Guy/Girl Relationships

help them grow. Commit to each other to be the kind of friends that sharpen each other, "Iron sharpeneth iron; so a man sharpeneth the countenance of his friend" (Proverbs 27:17).

5. Healthy friendships are a means to an end. Having a boyfriend or girlfriend is not the goal or destination of a wise Christian's life. Many young people think it should be.

The road that leads to marriage begins with real, authentic, godly friendships. For a Christian, youth should be a time when fellowship and time with godly friends provide a wealth of learning experiences that will one day be helpful in marriage and life. The moments you spend with friends in godly environments help you learn to relate, to mature, to connect, and to honor Christ.

One day you will use all of these collective experiences to choose a spouse and fulfill a life's call. In that moment, you will want to have no regrets regarding past friendships and relationships. You will want a clear conscience—a closet with no skeletons. Even more importantly, you will want to be the best spouse you can be. You will be thankful for godly friendships and how they contributed to helping you grow in God's grace.

6. Guy/girl attractions should be between Christians. Amos 3:3 teaches, "Can two walk together, except they be agreed?" Second Corinthians 6:14 says, "Be ye not unequally yoked together with unbelievers: for what fellowship hath righteousness with unrighteousness? and what communion hath light with darkness?"

This is really big! Guy/girl relationships among Christians are to be just that—"among Christians." God gives clear instructions in His Word that Christians are not to marry non-Christians. This means that Christians shouldn't even consider relationships with non-Christians. Light cannot have fellowship with darkness.

If you are serious about finding the *right person* at the *right time*, then you will be serious about *only* being attracted to Christians. Don't even entertain the idea of being attracted to a non-Christian. You will not reform them; they will reform you. We could both share dozens of stories of people who began relationships with non-Christians—at first hoping they could lead this person to Christ. The world's philosophy of "dating" is a terrible soulwinning strategy.

Along the same lines, wise Christians will only establish close friendships with *strong* Christians. If your friends don't have a heart for God, then they will only hurt you. It doesn't matter how cute someone is if they are leading you down the wrong path spiritually.

We've only begun to discover what a biblical friendship should look like. In the next chapter we'll take a closer look. For now, you probably need a break! This is a lot to digest, so go have a bowl of Lucky Charms and take a break. We will see you on the next page.

A Closer Look at Biblical Friendships

Have you ever really thought deeply about how friendships work? There is a lot more to friendships than just liking the same foods, playing the same sports, or using the same toothbrush. (Okay, that's just vile and random—no idea where it came from!)

Seriously, God has a great plan for friendships, and yet so often for young people, it's our friendships that become our downfall. So, whether you really are "just friends" or you actually kind of like each other and you're just telling everyone that you're "just friends"—there is a right way and wrong way to conduct a friendship. Let's break it down.

1. Biblical friendship involves three aspects of life. Christians consist of three parts—body, soul, and spirit.

25

Your body is the physical part of you. The Bible calls it your flesh, your tabernacle, and your members. It also calls your body the temple of the Holy Spirit (1 Corinthians 6:18–20). In other words, once you are saved, your body belongs to God.

Your soul is your mind, will, and emotions. It's your thinker, your chooser, and your feeler. It's the inner part of you that reasons through things, makes choices, and tells you how to feel at any given moment. The Bible often calls this your *heart*.

Your spirit is what was reborn when you trusted Christ as your Saviour. Your sin nature (or "old man") was crucified with Christ (Romans 6:6), and you became a new creature—a new man. The Holy Spirit of God came to take up residence inside of you. This gave you a new set of spiritual desires and the ability to know God and live His plan for your life. Read this statement carefully: You were once a *sinful creature* who was sometimes able to do right. Now you are a *righteous creature* who is sometimes able to sin. There's a very big difference!

Yes, you have all three parts, and all three play a role in friendships and guy/girl relationships.

Your body—When it comes to guy/girl relationships this is off limits. God says to save this completely for marriage. He says to flee youthful lusts (2 Timothy 2:22) and to flee fornication (1 Corinthians 6:18). Guaranteed, every time, if you get your body involved, you are headed down the wrong road—it leads to nowhere but pain. We'll see more about this in a coming chapter.

Your soul (mind, will, emotions)—In any friendship this plays a big part! This is where you determine your values, your character, and your feelings. This is where you make choices. In a guy/girl relationship your soul will contribute much, but it must be empowered and controlled by Someone greater than yourself. Unrestrained, your mind, your will, and your emotions will lead you in the wrong direction.

Your spirit (where friendships should begin)—Your spirit is what God will use to guide you in all of life—even one day in choosing a husband or wife. All friendships in life should be spiritual—the kind of friendships that are led of God's Spirit within you and where God and His Spirit are welcome.

In Ephesians 5, God commands us to be "filled with the Spirit." He desires for your life to be controlled and guided by His Holy Spirit, and that includes your friendships. Do you have spiritual friendships or carnal ones? Do your friends help you grow closer to God and encourage your walk with Him? If not, you need to ask God for some new friends.

2. Biblical friendship involves time together. Healthy, spiritual friendships develop the same way other friendships do—through time and attention. In other words, the more time you spend together and the more attention you give any friend (even when you're apart), the closer your friendship will become. This can be good, and it can be bad! In fact it can be *really* bad.

Between guys and girls, there's a healthy amount of time and attention to give to a friendship. Too much makes it too serious, too emotional, and too confusing. Too little makes it pointless. The problem is, none of us have a built-in gauge for reading how much time is too much time. You know—like your car has a gas gauge that tells you when you're running low. Wouldn't it be nice if we all had little gauges on our heads that flashed red lights when we spent too much time or gave too much attention to one person? It's not quite that easy—so we'll come back to this subject later.

The point here is, good friendships do involve the right amount of time and attention.

3. Biblical friends do wholesome things together. We live in a strange day. Many youthful friendships revolve around some really bad stuff—from music, to questionable places, to sexual talk, to satanic games and dirty social networking sites. This isn't friendship—it's just poison. Hanging out with these people doing and discussing these things isn't helping you, it's *rotting* you.

Godly people build their friendships in wholesome, pure, and Christ-honoring ways. We're talking about

Three—A Closer Look at Biblical Friendships

things like youth activities, church functions, and family outings. This might involve picnics, sports, miniature golf, restaurants, barbecues, putting puzzles together, playing board games, making popcorn, riding bikes, flying kites, and about a gazillion other things. There are many wholesome and fun ways to build good friendships.

4. Biblical friendships have purpose. Why do you have friends? So you can "fit in"? Because you need them? Everyone wants acceptance, but biblical friendships have a higher purpose than just hanging around and feeling cool. Biblical friendships are *headed somewhere*—they help you become a better person, and they compel you to go the right direction in life. Here are a few goals that should be the product of godly, encouraging friendships in your life—especially one with a "special someone."

1. To grow socially, emotionally, and spiritually
2. To become more like Christ
3. To help someone else grow spiritually
4. To have an enjoyable time and make good memories
5. To learn to love others selflessly
6. To learn to communicate with the opposite gender
7. To learn how to treat someone of the opposite gender
8. To learn how to keep Christ first in your life

9. To learn how to guard your heart
10. To prepare for your future

5. Biblical friendships have a good influence. Your friends impact you in a major way! You always become like them. You take on their reputation and people judge you by them. Your friends influence you in more ways than we could describe. In addition to this, your friendships influence other people—like your family, your siblings, your church family, your youth group, your pastor, and even your other friends.

> Choose friendships that help you grow.

For this reason, you should choose friendships that help you grow. Choose to be interested in people who have godly character and a good direction in life. Choose to hang around someone you would like to become more like—someone who will help you be more like Christ.

On top of this, don't have friends that your parents and spiritual authorities disapprove of. Parents and pastors can often see things you can't see. Your emotions can blind you, and don't forget the whole frontal lobe thing. Trust your parents and spiritual authorities, and let them direct your life into godly relationships. Here are a few reasons why:

1. God blesses those who honor authority. This principle always works—it's God's way of operating. When you honor and submit to authority, He honors and blesses you. Do

Three—A Closer Look at Biblical Friendships

you want things to "go well" with you in the future (Ephesians 6:3)? If so, then honor the authorities that God has placed in your life.

2. They have been where you are. You may not believe this, but your authorities know exactly how you feel when you are attracted to a guy or girl. They can help you survive this in a major way. They can help you establish right friendships, healthy attractions, and a hopeful future.

3. They have been down the "marriage road" where you are one day headed. Your spiritual authorities have experienced things you have not been confronted with yet. They know much more about love and relationships than you can possibly imagine. Let them help you read the road map to the *right person* at the *right time*.

4. They are wiser than you are. God has given your authorities wisdom for your life. And certain wisdom comes only with age. God designed for you to trust the wisdom of others as you grow—and for the rest of your life.

5. They care for your welfare. Believe it or not, your parents and pastors want the very best for you. Trust them. One day you will be exceedingly glad you did.

On a side note, we have dealt with many young adults who have been hurt, misled, or betrayed by so-called "authorities" somewhere in their past. God never intends for you to allow an authority figure to take His place in your life or to allow them to lead you in any direction that would go against His Word or His laws. No matter who in authority may have let you down, see God's bigger picture and don't let that disappointment keep you from God's best. Recognize that He has placed someone in your life to bless, guide, and strengthen you—someone you can trust. It may be a parent, a pastor, a grandparent, or a godly mentor. Whoever these people are, follow their faith as they follow the Lord. God blesses this pattern.

> It's not about dating; it's about maturing! It's not about falling in love; it's about growing in grace!

How far off are your philosophies from God's? Have you been buying into the world's thinking about dating and love? Have you been drawn down the wrong path by harmful friendships or relationships? Think about it. Do your friends strengthen your heart for God or weaken it? Are you a better son, daughter, brother, sister because of your friends? Do your friends help you respect your parents or tempt you to lie to them? Do your friends encourage you with spiritual talk, prayer, and uplifting attitudes? Or do they make you negative,

Three—A Closer Look at Biblical Friendships

ungrateful, cynical, and rebellious? Do you love God more or less because of their influence?

Take some time to review what we've studied. It's not about dating; it's about maturing! It's not about falling in love; it's about growing in grace! Good friendships help you grow. Good friends contribute positively to your spiritual life. Good friends make you a better person in every area.

God calls you to direct your attractions into godly friendships that will honor Him and help you prepare for an awesome future. God desires for you to learn from your friends and for them to learn from you.

Up until now, we've seen that there is definitely something special that God has created between guys and girls—regardless of what we call it. We've also seen that the young adult years come with many overwhelming changes and emotions, which makes it the wrong time for getting serious in a guy/girl relationship. And we've seen how good friendships can honor God and help your spiritual growth—even those with someone you are attracted to.

Let's move on and discover more about developing healthy relationships—especially those that involve sweaty palms.

Think About It
Chapters 1–3

Assignment for Personal Application

Find a quiet place, a blank paper, and think through these practical exercises. Consider sharing this exercise with a parent, friend, a group of friends, or a teacher.

1. List or describe the physical, emotional, and mental changes that you identified with the most.
2. In dealing with those changes, write out what you have been doing wrong, and what you need to begin doing faithfully.
3. Describe your four closest friendships. Are they carnal or spiritual friendships? Describe what you will personally do to make them more spiritual in the days ahead.
4. Write out a purpose statement for your goals in personal friendships. It should include the reasons why you desire friends, what kind of friends you will choose, and what kind of friend you will be. Make it a personal commitment to the Lord.
5. Are you building a good friendship with your parents? List three ways you can improve that relationship.

Memorize this verse: "Keep thy heart with all diligence; for out of it are the issues of life" (Proverbs 4:23).

Erasing Hollywood's Model

A major problem with the way we view relationships, love, and romance is that we've been unintentionally studying the wrong model. In the last chapter we saw God's model of biblical friendship. So now let's examine the wrong model of love. In other words, let's talk about how NOT to think!

Have you noticed how people in Hollywood can't stay married? It's never hard to find a magazine cover reporting about some movie star's sixth or seventh divorce, custody battle, or new dating relationship. Our secular culture is crazy about the search for true and lasting love—and they have *no clue* how to find it!

On top of that, the story lines of so many movies, TV shows, and novels—while entertaining—are far from truthful in presenting love and romance. Whether it's a

Disney princess or a popular actress, the story line is just about always the same. It goes something like this.

Love is mystical. It's purely chance and fate. It could happen at any time, and every heart longs for true love.

Love is a fleeting feeling. It could strike instantly, and when it does, you must follow your heart wherever love leads.

Love is a fantasy. When you find it, it will last forever, and you will live happily ever after.

Love is supreme. It doesn't matter if you need to run away, rebel against your parents, or lie, cheat and steal—just get love.

Love is essential. You must have it! No matter who you hurt, who you divorce, or who you abandon—follow love, for it may never return.

Love is now. No need to wait or prepare for true love. You can have it now while you are still young.

Love is sex. It's not about commitment or sacrifice. It's not about God. It's just about getting temporary pleasure for your body.

Love is all you need. No matter what's wrong in your life, love will fix it when you find the right person.

Love is a person. All of your life will be happy and peaceful when you fall in love with the *right person*.

Every one of these statements is a lie—and yet they are the central message of most entertainment media. If you've watched TV or a movie recently, you most likely heard this message, whether you realized it or not.

Four—Erasing Hollywood's Model

Think of sixteen or seventeen years of hearing that message over and over and over—maybe thousands of times. Combine that with a rewiring brain, an emotional world, and a twitterpated heart, and you could actually start to believe some of these lies. You could actually start trying to live in the fantasy of Hollywood rather than the reality of God's Word.

True love is not any of those things. In fact, those lies are the fastest path to a life of pain and disappointment—and no one better displays that than Hollywood personalities. What an odd thought. They can act it out on screen, but their reality is often the opposite.

Hollywood's Lie—Find the Right Person

The sum of Hollywood's model is simply this: *find the "right person."* Make yourself look good. Make yourself smell good. And then get out there and *find the "right person."* It's about finding that mystical moment with that dreamy person—that's when true love strikes.

And so, our world is filled with people looking for the *"right person."* They hang out at malls, visit night clubs, hit on people at bars, and even flirt with people at stoplights—all with the hopes of finding the *"right person."* When these things don't work, they try online dating sites, personality profiles, and compatibility tests. The heart cry is, "I MUST *find the 'right person'*!"

Then, when you find the *"right person,"* love takes over. You're supposed to go with what naturally happens at that point. Place all of your identity, your security, your needs, and your dreams into that person. Idolize them, live for them, and become completely emotionally dependent upon this *"right person."*

Naturally, this leads to being physical and to lies like, "If you love me then you will...." Inevitably this leads to sex before marriage which always leads to hurt and regret.

This is where the process starts to break down rapidly. God didn't design this process; therefore it never works. This model *always* fails. So, Hollywood's philosophy says, "When the model breaks down, go back to step one and start over again—go *find the 'right person.'*" In other words, you must not have had the *"right person"* to begin with, because *true* love mystically and magically works and it lasts forever.

So the world and Hollywood say, "If what you *thought* was true love doesn't last, walk away and go find the *'right person.'* It doesn't matter if you're married, if you have a family, or if you hurt someone—just go find true love while you can."

As a result, Hollywood places you on a downward spiral of failure—one of looking for the *"right person"* only to *never* find that person. After ten, twenty, or thirty years in this mess you will have a long trail of failed relationships, brokenness, and a trainwrecked life. What a blessing!

Four—Erasing Hollywood's Model

Remember this—Hollywood's model *never works*! It always breaks down. It always ends in disappointment. You will always come to failure if your hopes are attached to finding the *"right person"*—because even the *right person* will let you down. Then you'll think the answer is found in another *"right person."*

Don't buy Hollywood's lie. It never has worked, and it never will. To be sure, there is a *right person* for you. But there's something much more important than finding that person. We'll see this more in the next chapter.

How the World Affects Christians

"Love not the world, neither the things that are in the world. If any man love the world, the love of the Father is not in him" (1 John 2:15).

By the term *world,* God is not talking about the planet, but the "world system and philosophies" that Satan has embedded in the minds of people. He's referring to Hollywood's model of life. Just as God has given us His Word, laws, and commandments, Satan also has his philosophies—and they are always lies. Since the world is made up of mostly unsaved or non-Christian people, ungodly philosophies, habits, values, morals,

> Hollywood places you on a downward spiral of failure—one of looking for the "right person" only to never find that person.

and teachings are abundant. In the midst of all these, God calls us to be *in* this world but not to *love* it! He commands us to reject these lies and to base our lives upon His truth.

Inevitably, some of the world's philosophies are going to find their way into the subconscious mind whether by humanistic teaching in public schools, secular advertisements, radio, television, fashion, or music. Satan hammers you constantly to believe his lies. For this reason, as a Christian, you must always compare your thinking with God's—He calls this walking "circumspectly" (Ephesians 5). You must constantly check your heart and make sure you are not buying into Satan's lies.

James 4:4 says, "Ye adulterers and adulteresses, know ye not that the friendship of the world is enmity with God? whosoever therefore will be a friend of the world is the enemy of God."

How has the world affected Christians' philosophies on life and relationships? Let's consider several ways:

1. Wrong role models. The world would like to uplift sports and entertainment figures to be your role models in life. The entertainment industry—music, TV, and movies—almost always portrays immoral people as role models and moral people as stupid. Christians are usually depicted as fanatics, weirdos, hypocrites, or nuts.

Your role models ought to be those who are living in godliness and purity—those who love God and uplift His truth.

Four—Erasing Hollywood's Model

2. Wrong perspective on reality. Secular entertainment and news always feed on the *sensational*. They must create a sensational story—even if it's pure fantasy. Therefore, the message to our hearts is that anything in life short of spectacular is boring. This can cause us to lose touch with the everyday importance of reality in search of some fantasyland that doesn't exist.

3. Wrong view of love and marriage. Hollywood is fixated on immorality—sexual activity outside of marriage. It portrays this as expected and normal. Why does it take immodest ladies to sell cars or soft drinks? Because the world is desperately in search of fulfillment, and Satan is eager to pervert God's design for love, marriage, and the physical relationship. In the world's eyes, marriage doesn't work, and sex outside of marriage can be safe and fulfilling. It is neither safe nor fulfilling *ever*!

Hollywood's model of marriage and the home is directly opposed to God's model, and rarely, if ever, will you see an accurate depiction of a biblical home in secular media.

4. Wrong expectation of immediate gratification. To young people, someday seems far away—but it's not. In today's culture we're not interested in waiting for *anything*—whether it's a happy meal or a happy life. And the world says, "live for now—get all the pleasure and fun you can while you can." Most people are living for today with little thought of the consequences of their decisions. Immediate gratification teaches you to get what you want *now*, but God's Word makes it clear that the best things in life are worth waiting for!

Think of it this way—you will live the next fifty years with memories of how you lived as a young person. Live today in a way that will lead to no regrets.

5. Wrong emphasis on personal experience. God says "trust Me—live by faith." But the world says "try it, you might like it!" How many times have you heard a friend say, "I'll find out for myself"? This was Solomon's philosophy of life. Though he was the wisest man in history, he decided to give his heart to know folly and madness (Ecclesiastes 1:17). His life became a disaster as a result.

> God's Word makes it clear that the best things in life are worth waiting for!

This is the same thinking that the prodigal son had. He left "high-on-the-hog" and returned "lower than the hogs." The Scriptures say, "Touch not; taste not; handle not" (Colossians 2:21). But your world says the opposite. Society walks by sight and not by faith. This concept has led millions of young adults into drugs, alcoholism, immorality, abortions, murder, and homosexuality.

6. Wrong focus on fashion and the body. The world's fashions will always lead you to less modest clothing and more attention to your physical appearance. God tells us to focus on the "hidden man of the heart." First Peter 3 uses the word *adorning*. It refers to a decoration. In this passage, God teaches us that what

Four—Erasing Hollywood's Model

decorates us, or what makes us beautiful are the qualities of the heart—a meek and quiet spirit, humility, holiness, and godly character. Yet the world ignores these and places the focus only on outward decoration.

In the world's eyes, if it isn't "sexy" or "cool" then it isn't fashionable or attractive. Satan would love for you to ignore your heart and merely focus on trying to "fit in" with popular fashion trends. Don't fall into this trap. Let your godly character and your pure heart be your most important "decoration"!

7. **Wrong view of maturity.** In the world's eyes, the more knowledge you have of sin and the more experience you have with bad stuff, the more mature you are. If you don't know the meaning of bad words, if you don't get the punch-lines of dirty jokes, or if you don't catch the subtle meanings of innuendo, then you're just naive and stupid. The world scoffs at innocence. But again, this is a lie. Innocence is a thing of great value in God's eyes!

Romans 16:19 teaches us to be *simple* concerning evil and wise concerning good. In other words, be glad if you don't understand sin or wickedness. Be intentionally ignorant. Focus instead on growing in wisdom and in understanding that which is right and good.

Maturity is not familiarity with sin. Maturity is not an age. Maturity is *the acceptance of responsibility*.

The world would have every ten-year-old familiar with filthy words, sexual talk, and wicked lifestyles. The world would have every twelve-year-old girl in excessive makeup and high heels headed for trouble. Immorality abounds in today's culture because the world has forced a lie upon your generation.

Read back over these main points and think about them. The world's lies can really warp our thinking before we even realize it! Doesn't it bug you a little—or a lot—that Satan is so actively trying to mess with your heart and your values? We hope so!

The best thing you can do—erase these philosophies from your heart and life. Hollywood's model isn't working for *them*, and it will never work for *you*. It's flawed from the start.

The trouble is, most of us have been influenced more than we realize by Hollywood. The practice of *finding the right person* never works. It always breaks down. Why? Because God's philosophy is not about *finding* the right person. God will *lead you* to the right person.

God's plan is about *becoming* the right person—but that's for the next chapter. You're going to love this! Keep reading and let's discover God's way of preparing for *lifetime love*!

Discovering God's Model

Have you ever heard of a paradox? It's when something that seems contradictory isn't. It's when an illogical statement is actually true. And God's Word is full of them—like "the first shall be last" or "he that loses his life shall find it." God loves to take something illogical and prove our faith by working it out!

In Isaiah 55:8 God says, "my thoughts are not your thoughts, neither are your ways my ways." In other words, we don't think like God thinks and we don't act like God acts. This is also true in guy/girl relationships. When we understand how God thinks about these things, at first it doesn't make sense. But that's where living by faith comes in. When we trust and obey, He always works things out in our favor. Throughout God's Word He says "trust Me now—you'll understand later!"

This is one of those areas, so buckle up.

In the last chapter we saw that the world says, "Find the right person." This makes sense. And to say "finding the right person isn't about finding the right person" seems contradictory. If there *is* a right person, then wouldn't it be sensible to *find* that person?

But God's principle is a paradox. It goes like this: Finding the right person isn't about *finding* the right person—it's about *becoming* the right person!

Here's an illustration: I (Cary) recently helped my seventeen-year-old son get a car. It was a great privilege and blessing to be able to help make this happen. Why? Because he never asked for a car. He has been driving for over a year—his mom's minivan—and he's never expressed any discontentment. He doesn't even bug us about being able to drive a lot of places.

On top of this, he has a good testimony, he honors his mother and me, and he has lived with integrity in his friendships. He has worked, saved, and served as unto the Lord.

All of this made my wife and me eager to help him get a car. It would have been exactly the opposite if he had been nagging us constantly. His contentment with *not* having a car combined with his faithful life made us even more willing to bless him with one.

So it is with God and relationships. The more obsessed you are with *needing* a boyfriend or girlfriend, the more off-track you will get. The more you force your will on God, the less you will truly understand His will.

Five—Discovering God's Model

The more you search for the right person the farther you get from finding the right person! It doesn't make sense, but it's true.

Ephesians 5 is one of the great chapters in the Bible regarding marriage. But before the Holy Spirit ever mentions husbands and wives, He spends twenty-one verses on something more important. Before He teaches how to be a good husband or wife, He says, "Be ye therefore followers of God, as dear children; And walk in love..." (Ephesians 5:1–2).

> Finding the right person isn't about finding the right person—it's about becoming the right person!

He continues through the next verses to basically say "this is who you should be...." The chapter is all about being the right person—walking in light, understanding God's will, redeeming our time, being filled with the Holy Spirit.

It all starts with following God as a dear child and learning how to walk in love as Christ taught us. What does it mean to follow God as a dear child? It means you wrap your whole identity and security into Him. It means you see Him the way a little child sees a loving father. It means you journey through life with your hand clinging tightly to His (as opposed to a boy or girl), the way you walked through a shopping mall with your parents when you were four. It means that God holds all of your hopes and dreams—that He is your everything. It means that God is the center of your life—your provider, your strength, your refuge—not a boyfriend or girlfriend.

Only then can you grow in His grace and become the person He wants you to become. God says, before you become a husband or wife, focus your heart on following Him and walking in love. In other words, stop thinking about *finding* the right person and start thinking about *becoming* the right person. This is the reason that most high school romances go the wrong direction—they don't usually draw you closer to God, they *replace* Him! They cause you to seek what your heart needs from a girl or guy rather than from the Lord. This is bad because while you're getting to know another young person in a *wrong* way, you're NOT getting to know God the *right* way.

While the world would place you on a downward spiral of spiritual failure, God desires for you to be on an upward journey of spiritual growth.

You see, one day, when you are married, your marriage success will depend on your personal growth. It will depend on you changing and becoming the right person for your spouse.

When a marriage struggles—and all of them do—it doesn't mean you married the wrong person. It means you need to grow—to become a better person. Therefore, God says, focus on *becoming*. Focus on growing! This way, when a relationship breaks, you don't go find another person, you go back to following God and growing in His grace. It's an upward cycle of growth, and someday

Five—Discovering God's Model

in marriage you and your spouse will help each other on this growth journey. For this reason, your marriage will get better and better!

What does all this mean for your youth? It means God, not some pretend spouse, should be the *center* of your life. It means that you must spend more time preparing your heart than daydreaming about an infatuation. It means your *first love* should be Jesus Christ—not a boyfriend or girlfriend. It means that every friendship should be helping you *become* the person that God desires you to be.

Comparing the Two Models

Why is this important? Consider these contrasts between God's model and Hollywood's:

Becoming the right person places your hope in God. *Trying to find the right person* places your hope in another person.

Becoming the right person focuses on God's work in you. *Trying to find the right person* prevents God's work in you.

Becoming the right person makes you patient. *Trying to find the right person* makes you impatient.

Becoming the right person makes you strong. *Trying to find the right person* makes you weak.

Becoming the right person makes you spiritual. *Trying to find the right person* makes you self-centered and carnal.

Becoming the right person prepares you for the future. *Trying to find the right person* distracts you from growth.

Becoming the right person teaches you to trust God. *Trying to find the right person* teaches you to trust yourself.

Becoming the right person brings spiritual growth. *Trying to find the right person* brings disappointment.

Becoming the right person settles your emotions. *Trying to find the right person* confuses your emotions.

Becoming the right person makes you want to stay pure. *Trying to find the right person* tempts you to lose your purity.

Becoming the right person will make you a better spouse. *Trying to find the right person* will make you a worse spouse.

Becoming the right person will lead you to the right person. *Trying to find the right person* will lead you astray.

Becoming the right person places your emotional stability in God. *Trying to find the right person* makes you emotionally unstable.

Becoming the right person seeks love and acceptance from God. *Trying to find the right person* seeks love and acceptance from people.

Five—Discovering God's Model

Becoming the right person makes God your strength. *Trying to find the right person* seeks strength from another person.

Someday, when you are married, following God's model will hold your marriage together, and following Hollywood's model will break it apart. Hollywood says, "Go find another person." God says, "Stay with your spouse and become the right person." One model says, "If I grow and become the right person, this relationship will become better." The other model says, "I've got the wrong person. I need to ditch this relationship and go find a better one!"

With this in mind, when is the best time to start becoming the right person? It's like that question: When is the best time to plant a tree? The answer: ten years ago. When is the second-best time to plant a tree? Today! So it is spiritually. The best time to start becoming the right person is ten years ago. The second-best time is today!

Here's the big point of all this, so don't miss it.

During these years you will either focus on *becoming* the right person or *finding* the right person. Not only is finding the right person a losing proposition—it's too early anyway! So it's a complete and total waste of time. Sadly, most youthful guy/girl relationships fall into this category—a complete waste of time. But they don't have to. There is a way to establish godly guy/girl friendships and keep them from going this direction.

If you will focus on becoming the right person, every friendship will have a godly purpose and a Christ-centered approach. Every relationship—whether there is attraction or not—will be directed to the Lord and guided by His Word. Every friendship will be the kind that helps you grow and prepare for your future.

We've seen Hollywood's model and God's model—finding the right person versus becoming the right person. Which way are you thinking? Why are you "just friends" with someone of the opposite gender? Is it so you can have security, acceptance, and artificial love? Is it so you can pretend to be married? Or is it so you can grow in God's grace and prepare for the right person in your future.

God's Model in Action

One of the best examples of God's model in action is found in Genesis 24 in the love story of Isaac and Rebekah. It's one of the great love stories of the Bible. Let's review it for a moment.

Isaac is a godly young man. We know this because he was willing to lay down his life in sacrifice to the Lord. He was also willing to trust his father when it came to girls and marriage. He trusted the Lord, honored his parents, and walked with God. He was mature enough to understand his need to meditate and be alone with God.

Rebekah was also a godly young woman. She was pure, she was a hard worker, and she too honored and trusted her parents. She had a servant's heart and a godly demeanor.

Both Isaac and Rebekah were living contented and mature lives. Neither were "boy-crazy" or "girl-crazy." They were both "God-crazy." They were living their lives for God and growing in His grace. They were patient to wait on His timing. Their story reveals two people who were *focused* on becoming the right person. And though they were miles apart, God used amazing circumstances to bring them together, and it was love at first sight—for the rest of their lives! It truly is an amazing story.

Contrast this with Samson—who was busy trying to find the right person. He rejected God's plan, rebelled against his parents, and flat out told them which girl to "get" for him. His statement was basically, "Go get her for me; she pleases me!" Boy was he wrong! In fact he was beyond wrong—he was disastrously wrong, and his life never did recover.

Do you want an *Isaac and Rebekah life* or a *Samson and Delilah life*? That's a no-brainer. God's way—though a paradox—is always the best. You find the right person by becoming the right person. It's that simple.

During youth, while there's nothing wrong with being attracted to a guy or girl, it's extremely important that those attractions become friendships of spiritual growth. It is vital that they not become consuming, idolatrous, or emotionally dependent. Your life must be consumed with God and dependent upon Him, and your friendships and relationships should help you grow in His grace.

The really cool part is that God has a very special way of preparing you for and making you the right person. Keep reading, we're going to study that next.

six

A Wonderful "Someday!"

Consider a very serious question. Do you want a wonderful "someday"? Do you want a future that unfolds better than you could imagine? That's what God desires to give you. First Corinthians 2:9 says, "But as it is written, Eye hath not seen, nor ear heard, neither have entered into the heart of man, the things which God hath prepared for them that love him." God is working on your *someday*, and you're going to love it!

Everything you do today is about *preparing* for your future. That's what youth is all about. God compares your youth to planting seeds. He says in Psalm 1 that if you will choose the right friends, hang around the right crowd, and plant yourself into His Word, then one day (in the right season) you will bear fruit! In Galatians 6 the Bible calls this "sowing and reaping." *Sowing* is planting seeds, and *reaping* is harvesting the fruit of what you planted. Some people think of sowing and reaping as a *negative*—and some as a *positive*. I guess it's all about what you're planting. If you're planting good seeds, you're going to reap a good harvest. If you're planting trash, then yes, you should be *very afraid*, because harvest time will eventually come, and there will be no undoing the damage that you have done.

The struggle with sowing and reaping is *the wait*! Most people get tired of waiting. Again, we want immediate gratification—instant results. We struggle with seeing the value of waiting for God's timing. And, on the other hand, those who are sowing bad stuff start to believe that they are getting away with it—which is never the case.

The Truth of Sowing and Reaping

Consider these important truths about sowing and reaping:

    1. **Harvest always comes.** There's no avoiding it. Nobody beats this principle.

    2. **Harvest always requires a wait.** There's always a gap between planting the seed and reaping the harvest. Usually the wait is years, not months.

    3. **Harvest requires tenacity.** Like the little fish in *Finding Nemo*, just keep sowing, just keep sowing, just

Six—A Wonderful "Someday!"

keep sowing. Keep sowing the right seeds and don't get weary with well-doing.

4. Harvest always reflects the seed. You get what you plant. If you plant sin, you reap the damage. If you plant good character, you reap the blessings.

5. Harvest always involves outside forces. Like the sun and rain affect the farmer's seeds, so your friends, your church, your influences (music, entertainment, etc.), and your daily lifestyle impacts the seeds you're planting.

Remember, everything you're doing right now is about *preparing* for your future. In every area of life, you are sowing seeds—and one day you will reap a harvest. God says in Galatians 6:9, "And let us not be weary in well doing: for in due season we shall reap, if we faint not."

Do you want a great marriage someday? Do you want an awesome future? Do you want God to exceed your expectations and hopes? Remember—God's model is "become the right person." A wonderful *someday* is about sowing right seeds *today*!

> In every area of life, you are sowing seeds—and one day you will reap a harvest.

If you were to plant a peach pit and grow a peach tree, it would take a couple of years before you even had a seedling tree strong enough to survive in a garden or orchard. After you planted your young tree in an orchard, you would need to wait about three more years before you could get fruit from that peach tree. Though it would try to grow fruit, you would need to pull it off early so that the nutrients would remain in the tree to strengthen it. After about five years, your tree would finally be ready to grow full-size peaches. If you rush the cycle or refuse to wait, your tree will never bear peaches in the amount or the size that it could have. Reaping fruit too early would forever limit the fruit of the tree and stunt its growth.

The same is true in your life. If you rush God's timing, get into serious relationships too soon, and try to reap fruit too early, you will forever change what your life could have been.

Having a wonderful *someday* is about two very important things. Let's take a look at them:

A Wonderful "Someday" Comes by Sowing the Right Seeds

You will never have a wonderful "someday" if you don't start planting the right seeds now. The problem with modern marriages and families is that people think a good marriage happens automatically—again, like love is some mystical fantasy over which you have no control.

Love is a choice—you plant it, grow it, harvest it. Just like carrots! You don't do a mystical rain-dance and quote magic spells to grow carrots. You just plant the right seeds in the right environment, protect them from

Six—A Wonderful "Someday!"

Bugs Bunny, and let them grow. Carrots *will happen*. There's no doubt and no mysticism to it.

That's how love is. That's how a great marriage happens—by choice. It's a decision that starts now—long before you're married. It's a course you decide to take long before you arrive at the destination. If you want to arrive someday at a lifetime love and great marriage, you have to get the road map and start the journey in the right direction.

So, what seeds do you plant to grow a great lifetime love? Do you plant dating seeds? Kissing seeds? Hand-holding seeds? What kind of seeds will eventually reap the harvest of true love? Well, it's simple. Let's start at the harvest and work backwards. Let's take a look at what makes a great marriage, and then we'll know what seeds to plant now.

1. A great marriage is made of TRUST. Trust is about believing and relying upon your spouse. It is about being believable and trustworthy yourself. If you don't have trust in your marriage, we promise you, kissing will be out of the question!

What seed grows the fruit of trust? That's easy—*truthfulness*. So start planting the seeds of honesty in your life. Be truthful. Be real. In other words, if you are really good at lying, hiding the truth, and sneaking around the rules—you're planting the wrong seeds and harvest time will not be fun.

2. A great marriage is made of COMMITMENT. Failure is not an option. Marriage is a lifetime commitment, but commitment doesn't just grow instantly because we repeated a vow and ate wedding cake. Commitment is something that grows from the right seed.

What seed grows the fruit of commitment? *Surrender*. If you will surrender your life to Christ right now, you are practicing the skill of commitment for your future family. If you can't trust God with your life and commit completely to Him, you will never commit completely to another human being—no matter what you say in the wedding ceremony. Start living a surrendered life to Christ—commit fully to Him—and you're heading directly into the harvest of commitment in marriage. Isn't that cool?!

3. A great marriage is made of INTIMACY. Intimacy means "just the two of us." When you get engaged someday, your future spouse will not want all of your former boyfriends or girlfriends coming along for the date. That would be the opposite of intimate! The greatest of marriages is where intimacy is truly just the two of us!

What seed grows the fruit of intimacy? *Purity*. You grow intimacy in your marriage by planting purity in your youth—by reserving yourself for just one person—physically and emotionally.

4. A great marriage is made of LOVE. I don't mean the fantasyland kind. I mean the giving kind. True love is a choice to give. True love is sacrificial and lives for the honor of another.

Six—A Wonderful "Someday!"

What seed grows the fruit of love? *Loving Christ*. You don't practice marital love by dating lots of people before marriage. You practice marital love by loving God first and foremost. When you choose to love Christ, His love will find its way out of your heart toward others.

5. A great marriage is made of SUBMISSION. In Ephesians 5, God tells us to submit ourselves to each other, and then wives to submit to husbands. Submission is learning to give in. Submission is letting another person win. Submission is saying, "I'll let your desires become mine, and I'm happy to let you have your way." Great marriages are made of two people who know how to give in to each other. But most young adults spend a good amount of time fighting for their way—wrong seed!

What seed grows the fruit of submission? *Selflessness*. You learn to submit by learning to give in. In other words, if you are a selfish brat at home right now, you're going to be a selfish brat of a spouse. If you think everybody else's rules are stupid, you'll think your spouse is stupid too. But if you plant the seeds of selflessness—if you begin learning to let others have their way and to sacrifice yourself for someone else—you are preparing for a great harvest. The Bible says it this way, "Be kindly affectioned one to another with brotherly love; in honour preferring one another" (Romans 12:10).

You see, you don't prepare for a great marriage by writing love notes in Algebra class or by standing in a dark corner goo-goo eyed at each other. You don't prepare for marriage by making out or being flirtatious. You don't prepare for marriage by being immoral or saying "I love you" to fifteen different people during your young adult years.

You prepare for a wonderful *someday* by planting the seeds that make a great marriage. What seeds are you planting? Remember, harvest time will come, and you will live with what you plant. Maybe it's time to start seriously planting the right seeds!

A Wonderful "Someday" Comes by Waiting for the Right Season

Many young people have said, "I'm tired of being good." We don't blame you. There truly is a burden that comes with planting good seeds. It's hard work, and sometimes you just get tired of trying. We all do. That's when you have to step back and think about harvest time. The work is worth it!

Think about a farmer who gets up early for many spring days and works the fields. First he prepares the soil; then he plants the seed; and then he spends long hours over hard months nurturing and protecting the seed. Do you think that might get tiring? Of course. But harvest time makes it all worthwhile.

That's why God reminds us not to grow weary. He must have anticipated that we might! Do yourself a favor sometime—look up all the times the word *patience*

Six—A Wonderful "Someday!"

is used in the Bible. You'll be amazed. Patience is one of God's big requirements—He likes to work by *His* timetable, and He's not in a hurry. He's more concerned with who you are becoming than how fast you are getting there. His work takes time—that's how He's planned it. In Philippians 1:6, He actually says that His good work in you will take the *rest of your life*. Talk about patience! We want God to finish His work on us *yesterday*!

> You prepare for a wonderful someday by planting the seeds that make a great marriage.

The point is, the best marriages come to those who during their youth were willing to wait on God's timing. We do a lot of marriage and premarital counseling, and the happiest couples are always those who spent their younger years patiently planting and looking forward to harvest. They didn't rush dating. They didn't lose their purity. They didn't break all the rules, sneak around their parents, and plant all the wrong seeds. They just planted good stuff and nurtured it—day after day, year after year. And in God's time—"in His season"—harvest came and the wait was well worth it. We have *never* had a patient couple who came back and said, "We sure wish we hadn't waited!" All of them say, "We're so glad we did wait!"

Let's just be honest—waiting is a *royal pain*. But it's worth it! Don't try to get fruit from a tree that isn't ready. Plant your heart in the Word of God and let God bring forth fruit in the right season. Let Him grow you in patience, and let patience have her perfect work (James 1:4) so that you can be mature and ready for what lies ahead.

Very few people actually prepare for marriage, and even fewer prepare early. Usually young adults are too wrapped up in wrong relationships to focus on "becoming the right person." The best time to prepare for a great marriage is right now, and the way to prepare is to sow the seeds that will reap a wonderful *someday*. It's a no-brainer, but very few actually get this!

A few final thoughts.

You will be attracted to someone like yourself. If you are planting lies, you will probably be attracted to someone who is doing the same. This makes for a really bad combination. One reason to *become* the right person is so you will be attracted to someone with right qualities, and they will be attracted to you. Extreme illustration: Drug dealers aren't usually attracted to narcotics officers.

You will become more like the person to whom you are attracted. Not only does character attract, but it is also contagious. Spiritual people influence their friends to greater spiritual growth. Good qualities are contagious, just like bad qualities are contagious. If you want to develop rotten character, then hang around people with rotten character. If you want to become the right person, then find someone you can be like and hang around them!

Six—A Wonderful "Someday!"

There's just something about a *wonderful someday* that makes you want to get there in one piece! Let's take a break, and we'll see you in part two!

The Seeds of a Wonderful "Someday"

Sow	Reap
Truthfulness	Trust
Surrender	Commitment
Purity	Intimacy
Loving Christ	Love
Selflessness	Submission

Think About It
Chapters 4–6

Assignment for Personal Application

Find a quiet place, a blank paper, and think through these practical exercises. Consider sharing this exercise with a parent, friend, a group of friends, or a teacher.

1. Describe three ways you have recently seen "Hollywood's model" being communicated.

2. What are some things you can actively do to counteract or erase Hollywood's model from your heart and thinking? List four or five things and commit to doing them.

3. Describe a paradox and explain why you believe God uses paradoxes to teach us His principles.

4. In a few paragraphs, describe God's model and why you believe it is better than Hollywood's model.

5. Slowly read Genesis 24 and list all the examples or principles of God's model that you can find in this chapter.

6. Describe whether you are sowing the seeds of good character or bad character and in what ways.

Memorize these verses: "Love not the world, neither the things that are in the world. If any man love the world, the love of the Father is not in him" (1 John 2:15).

"But as it is written, Eye hath not seen, nor ear heard, neither have entered into the heart of man, the things which God hath prepared for them that love him" (1 Corinthians 2:9).

PART TWO
Make Big Choices

To arrive at a "wonderful someday" we must make some big choices. In the coming chapters we will study those choices and challenge you to do the right thing now so God can bless your future!

SEVEN

Choose "The Right Person at the Right Time"

The goal of any friendship or guy/girl relationship should be to help you become the person that God wants you to be. And yet, as we've seen, many friendships and relationships do exactly the opposite. Relationships that should strengthen and prepare us, in today's culture, often turn into emotional nightmares filled with sexual risks, frustration, disappointment, confusion, and misery.

Wouldn't you like to do this differently? It is possible to have a friendship with the opposite gender in a way that honors the Lord. It's all about right choices! In the next few chapters, we will explore the choices you must make to have healthy guy/girl relationships during your youth.

These choices are tough in today's culture, but those who have the courage to make them always end up with better lives, better marriages, and happier hearts.

The first and most important choice: be committed to *the right person at the right time.*

Stay Focused on the Goal

You must choose a wonderful someday and stay focused on it through all of your youthful friendships. It's not about falling in love *now*—it's about preparing now for *the right person at the right time.*

Think about that—*the right person at the right time*! Say it five times in your head. If you only remember one thing from this book remember this—*the right person at the right time.* You must get there! But you must there God's way—it's the only way.

If it's God's will for you to one day be married, there is a right person for you! Only God really knows who that person is and when you will meet. He's preparing *that person* for you and *you* for that person. In time, He will intersect your lives by His providential will. The question is not: will you *find* that person? The question is: will you be *ready* for that person? Will you give that person the best spouse possible?

One of Satan's desires is to prevent that relationship from happening, or to damage *it* by damaging *you*. Many young adults in today's culture are throwing away all chances of having a lifetime love by sowing seeds of

Seven—The Right Person at the Right Time

destruction now. By giving their hearts and bodies away prematurely they are killing any chance of a happy someday. It's a cheap trick. Satan offers a dollar's worth of pleasure now, but you trade ten million dollars' worth of lifetime love! It's just not worth it.

Do you remember Esau? The Bible calls him *profane* in Hebrews 12:16. He traded his birthright for one bowl of soup. What a complete idiot! God had a lifetime of blessings and fulfillment, but Esau let momentary hunger control his thinking. He was the *king* of immediate gratification. He wanted satisfaction *now*, no matter what it cost. And so, he traded all the future blessings of God for a full stomach. What was he thinking?

Actually, he wasn't thinking. That's the problem. His reasoning was warped. His frontal lobe must not have formed properly. He lost sight of the long term—the big picture. He forgot the goal. He let a physical craving kill his lifetime vision. Sounds like many young people today.

God says in Proverbs 29:18, "Where there is no vision, the people perish...." In this verse the word *vision* refers to a revelation from God through His Word. Vision is *a mental image of God's preferred future*. It's God's intention for your future, and if you live in God's will, it's not a *maybe* proposition, it's a *definite*! Do you have God's vision for your future? Or are you more like Esau—needing immediate gratification, even if it costs you all of God's blessings?

Too many today are *profane* in their thinking—their logic and reasoning don't make sense. They are chasing short-term pleasure and sacrificing long-term vision. They are trading God's best for less than one full stomach.

So, what will compel you to stay pure for your future spouse? What will empower you to control your physical cravings now? *A clear picture of God's vision*—the right person at the right time.

Capture God's Vision

It's time to make a major philosophical shift in your thinking. It's time to align your thoughts with God's thoughts. It's time to capture God's long-term vision—to see His big-picture perspective. Nothing will enable you to stay pure like having the end in mind!

Your friendships are not about immediate gratification. They mustn't be! You must lift your head, look farther down the road, and see where you're headed. If you go too far, too fast, too soon with your "just friends" attractions, you will end up in a mess. But if you keep the end goal in view—the right person at the right time—you'll develop friendships that help you stay on course.

God has a right person, and He has a right time. And we hate to break this to you—you most likely don't even know the right person yet. And your teen years are

Seven—The Right Person at the Right Time

definitely not the right time, even if you do know the right person.

The formula is twofold! In other words, it's possible to have the right person at the wrong time or in the wrong way. God's ultimate vision for your guy/girl relationships is to preserve, protect, and prepare you for the right person at the right time.

You must choose to live with this perspective. Every friendship is either making you *more* prepared for the right person or *less* prepared. Every note, email, text message, or phone call is either strengthening you for the journey or weakening you.

Are you on God's path of preparation for the right person, or are you taking a massive detour away from the right person? The Holy Spirit will answer this in your heart if you will face the truth and deal with it.

> God's ultimate vision for your guy/girl relationships is to preserve, protect, and prepare you for the right person at the right time.

You must have God's vision and you must not trade it for *anything*! It's not worth giving away for a kiss, for a night, for a date, or for the fleeting feeling of artificial love. God's blessing on your future is worth the wait. Don't play the Esau game—it will only lead to hurt and regret. Don't trade a lifetime of love for a dollar's worth of pleasure now. Don't let a momentary physical craving kill your ability to think clearly.

Keep your heart focused on this thought—the right person at the right time. Keep reminding yourself—no matter how much I like *this* person, I don't know for sure if this is the right person, and this definitely isn't the right time. So for now, I'm still preparing, growing, and getting ready. This friendship should help me grow. If it doesn't, then I must let it go.

Knowing the Right Person at the Right Time

How will you know the right person and the right time? That's a reasonable question, and this is a reasonable age to start grasping what the right person and the right time will look like. We share these thoughts not so you can find the right person *now*, but rather so you can develop the right thought process.

The right person will have four basic dynamics that align with God's principles. These are not original with us. We've both heard them from a variety of sources over the years, but they make a lot of sense. The right person will have these four values in place:

1. Character. This is a heart for God and a committed life. This is a life that is growing in biblical wisdom and understanding. This is a heart of integrity and honesty. Many people follow after outward attraction or beauty with little thought of character. Think of it this way. If this person is lying, cursing, and throwing furniture at you one day, you won't really

Seven—The Right Person at the Right Time

care how handsome or beautiful he or she is! The right person will be a person of strong character. This is the first thing to find out about a person—long before you ever get into a serious relationship.

2. Competence. This is the ability to grow in knowledge. Does this person have the capacity to learn the basic skills of marriage—building a home, leading a family, and loving a spouse? For instance, it really won't matter how funny or cute Norbert is if he can't keep a job, pay the rent, or put food on your table.

Everybody has areas of incompetence, but the question is, can this person grow into responsibility? Does he or she have the basic raw qualities of competence that marriage and family life require?

3. Chemistry. This is the friendship factor. It's usually what we focus on in the short term, but it's bigger than short term. Do I *really like* this person or do I just like *being liked*? Eight out of ten high school relationships are more about *being liked*! Chemistry is simply this: can this person be my absolute best friend for life? Do our hearts click with a kind of closeness that time will only strengthen? Or does this person irritate, annoy, and frustrate me? While every relationship struggles, the right person will be your absolute, lifetime companion and best friend, and time will only make that union better.

4. Will of God. This is the final factor in the equation: is this person God's will for me? If character is solid, competence is in place, and chemistry is growing, the last piece of the puzzle is simply to prove whether God's will includes this person.

This begs the question—how do I know when a person is God's will for me? Ah, now that deserves its own chapter! We'll cover that next.

In summary, if you want to have a right relationship, you must make right choices. The first right choice which we've seen in this chapter is be committed to *the right person at the right time*. Choose God's best over immediate gratification.

Let's take a look at the second choice.

Choose God's Will

The second choice necessary for healthy relationships is simply this—*stay in the will of God, no matter what!*

The most common question we are asked by Christian young people is this, "How do I know the will of God?" What they normally mean is, "How do I know the *future* will of God right *now*." Unfortunately, God doesn't work that way. He doesn't give out information about His will until you need to know it and until He's certain that you are already surrendered to it—no matter what. He doesn't give out information to be considered among other options. He reveals His will to those who say "YES" before they know what it is. And the way to say "YES" to the future will of God is to say "YES" to His will today.

Years ago I (Mike) heard a camp evangelist tell the story of courting his wife while in Bible college. After being engaged they were reviewing their separate spiritual journeys. She asked what year he accepted Christ, and he told her. She said, "That's the same year I dedicated my life to do God's will." She asked with a grin, "What month was it?" He replied. She said, "That's the same month I decided to do His will." With excitement in her voice she asked, "What day was it?" He told her. Shocked, she said, "That was the very day I knelt to give Jesus my all." "What time was it?" she slowly asked. He gave the time. Believe it or not, at the exact time she was surrendering to do God's will, her future husband was kneeling at a church altar getting saved. God was working behind the scenes to place them both on the path of a wonderful someday, and it hinged on their choice for God's will during their younger years.

God's Will for Today

The road to God's *someday will* starts with His *today will*. It starts right in front of you, choosing the right things right now. Before you can know God's future will, you have a choice *today* regarding what you already know is God's will—are you doing it?

Our lives are the sum total of the decisions we make—like lined up dominoes, every small decision affects the next one. Little by little, one decision at a

Eight—Choose God's Will

time, we put together a life—either in God's will or out of it.

Therefore, it is vital that you stay in God's will through your young adult years. Every friendship is either a step into His will or a step away.

Living in God's will takes commitment. If you are passionate about being right with God, you will most likely say *no* to some guy/girl relationships, and *yes* to others. And you won't be desperate either way. You will either be more focused on *finding* a boyfriend or girlfriend or on *staying* in the will of God.

Are you committed to staying in God's will even if that doesn't include a boyfriend/girlfriend right now? If you're willing to leave God's will for a friend, this must change *right now*. Choose God's will, no matter what.

> Every friendship is either a step into His will or a step away.

Let's take a little test. Think about your present friendships and guy/girl interactions and ask yourself these questions:

Are my relationships keeping me in God's will or leading me out of it? Do they please the Lord or dishonor Him? Do they honor my parents' guidelines or break them? Do my friends help me stay pure or tempt me to give in? Are they spiritually minded or suggestive, flirtatious, and sensual?

How do my relationships affect my lifestyle and daily schedule? Do I spend time with God before I give time to a guy or girl? Am I seeking to know God more than I'm seeking to know my friend? Am I serving the Lord in some way or living for a special someone?

Do I make God's simple commands a higher priority in life than my heartthrob? Am I living for Christ or for a person? Am I living uprightly before Him or hiding sin from Him? Am I real or phony?

If you are out of God's will now, not only are you unhappy, but you'll only be more unhappy in the future! The most miserable place to be is outside of God's will.

Getting out of God's will starts with little decisions that lead to big backsliding. It happens gradually—one small step at a time.

If we sent a rocket to the moon, but altered the course by just two degrees, we would not only miss the moon, but we'd miss it by tens of thousands of miles. That's how God's will is. If you alter your course as a young adult by just small increments—like two degrees—you will miss the someday will of God by a great distance.

How Young Adults Leave God's Will

There are three very common things which often lead people out of the will of God. This list could be much longer, but these are the things we see Satan use over and over. Guard your heart in these matters:

1. A serious dating relationship. Too often these take the place of God and cause a person to be too involved, move too fast, and go too far. The message of this book is to *keep it light* and keep *it right*!

2. A new job. Whether it's the crowd at work, the music we hear, or the temptation to miss church for work, jobs often tempt young adults to leave God's will. It boils down to loving money more than God. We hope that your relationship with God is worth more than minimum wage! And by the way, minimum wage jobs are very easy to find, so find one that won't require you to work on Sunday. Keep God first.

3. A new friend. When you start a new friendship, you must quickly evaluate the spiritual temperature of this person. If you sense that this person will not strengthen you in the Lord, then keep it as a casual acquaintance. Choose spiritual people to be your closest friends. No need to be mean or rude—just don't be close.

God says in 1 John 2:17, "And the world passeth away, and the lust thereof: but he that doeth the will of God abideth for ever." In other words, a lustful relationship is destined for a train wreck, but a relationship in God's will has eternal value!

Many years ago, there was a wonderful young lady in my (Mike) youth group who was very committed to Christ. She never became boy-crazy because she was more focused on knowing and living for God. She invested her life into others as a servant-hearted Christian rather than becoming self-focused on having boyfriends and being liked.

After graduating from college she entered the ministry to serve at a troubled girls' home. I had heard a good looking, spiritual guy was very interested in her. The next time I saw her, I asked her about this young man. She said, "We ended that friendship, I sensed a reserve. If he wouldn't give his whole life to Jesus, how could I trust him to give his whole life to me?"

This young lady had an amazing perspective of God's will for *someday*! She knew that it was better to wait for the right person than to be desperate for *any* person. She chose the will of God for today, and ultimately God gave her the right person at the right time. Now she's enjoying a blessed life, but it all started with a tough choice to stay in God's will.

> God's primary way of blessing a young person is through honor and obedience to parents.

Discerning God's Will

How does God speak today? How do we know His will? Right now is a great time to learn how to hear God's voice in your life. If you choose to stay in His will, then you'll need to listen carefully to His voice. There are five primary ways that God speaks to His people today. Let's study them briefly so you can learn to hear Him when He leads you:

1. His Word. This is the final authority for all of God's "speaking." God never contradicts His Word. The more you know the Bible and apply its truth, the more you will recognize God's voice. For this reason, it is vital that you study His Word and go to Him with all of your questions. Most young people take their confusion to friends who are just as confused. That's a mistake. Learn to go to God's Word. There's no better way to hear His voice.

2. His appointed authorities. In every life, God makes His will known through the guidance of biblical authorities. You will *never* outgrow this, and you shouldn't want to. In most of the practical areas of life—like girl/guy relationships—God's will can be clearly seen by asking these questions: What do my parents want me to do? What are my youth group's rules, etc.?

God's primary way of blessing a young person is through honor and obedience to parents (or spiritual authority if parents are absent). That's why He said in Ephesians 6:3, "That it may be well with thee...." Doesn't everybody hope for a life that goes *well*? For a young adult, especially a teen, that life is always a product of obeying authority. Get in the habit of trusting your parents and spiritual leaders—this is one way God keeps people in His will.

3. His Holy Spirit within. When you trusted Christ, God placed His Holy Spirit in you (Ephesians 1:13, 1 Corinthians 6:19–20). And in Ephesians 5:18 we are commanded to be filled with the Spirit. God also instructs us to quench not and grieve not the Holy Spirit (1 Thessalonians 5:19, Ephesians 4:30). All of this shows that God desires to direct our lives moment by moment. Dr. Paul Chappell often says, "Obey every impulse of the Holy Spirit."

Ask God to help you hear and obey the Holy Spirit. This is a life-long process, but hearing and obeying His promptings will cause you to make hundreds of right decisions while you are young.

4. His Spirit-led counselors. God's Word says in Proverbs 15:22, "Without counsel purposes are disappointed: but in the multitude of counsellors they are established." God often speaks to us and confirms His will through the voices of others. In addition to parents and pastors, God places wise people in our lives—teachers, mentors, and godly friends.

A wise person learns to listen to the advice and counsel of others—especially when a circumstance is filled with emotions and potential risk. For instance, if you have an interest in someone, but the wise people in your life are cautioning you, you would be wise to listen to their counsel. We'll see in the next chapter that it is easy to be blinded by emotions and personal desires. We can even attach spiritual labels to very unspiritual decisions by saying things like, "I've prayed about this."

This is where getting advice comes in. Can you admit when you are "in over your head"? Can you admit that some life circumstances are too emotional or beyond your wisdom? Then depend on the advice of godly people. People with great lives didn't get there

Eight—Choose God's Will

by accident. They got there by listening to a lot of good advice.

Find people who are where you want to be spiritually and ask them for directions on how to get there! That's what getting counsel is all about.

5. His providential circumstances. God uses circumstances to point us to His will, but we usually fail to tie the circumstances to His purpose. Sometimes we're more focused on *changing* our circumstances than on *hearing* His voice and learning from those circumstances. In every circumstance, you should ask, "God, what are you telling me through these circumstances?"

> People with great lives didn't get there by accident. They got there by listening to a lot of good advice.

When it comes to *someday* and the right person, you will definitely want to see God's hand orchestrating the circumstances in your life. Again, Isaac and Rebekah are a good example of this—God was *obviously* working things out for them. Circumstances were one of the ways they understood His will.

Whatever your circumstances are right now, they are ordered and allowed by God. It's been said this way: whatever is *outside* of your control is *in* the will of God. Romans 8:28 promises that God is always doing something good through our circumstances if we love Him and live according to His purpose.

Keeping Your Friendships in God's Will

Friendships that eventually lead to marriage are a part of God's will. He has already decided which girl or guy He wants you to eventually fall in love with and marry. Many marry people they never thought they would as they began their friendship. For this reason, focusing on being friends rather than being boyfriend/girlfriend is actually a really good idea. It is wise to establish great friendships in God's will—one of them may prove to be the seeds of a wonderful lifetime companionship.

As we close this chapter, let's think about some practical ways to keep your friendships, especially guy/girl relationships, in the will of God:

1. Pray daily for wisdom. Philippians 4:6, "Be careful for nothing; but in every thing by prayer and supplication with thanksgiving let your requests be made known unto God." Ask God daily to help you honor Him in your relationships.

2. Pray for the person God is preparing for you. Ask God to keep your future spouse in His will. Ask Him to make you the right person as well.

3. Predetermine what kind of close friends you will have. Remember, God's will for your life is at stake—it is sacred! You will someday marry a friend. For this reason, be courageous enough to separate from bad influences and establish good ones—even if you are ridiculed or rejected in the process. You don't owe bad

Eight—Choose God's Will

friends an explanation, just kindly walk away with a good attitude.

4. Pray for and with your friends. Don't be afraid to bring your walk with God into your daily friendships. Christian friends should be able to encourage each other, pray together, and share what they are learning from God's Word. Are you more comfortable talking about a movie or TV show than you are talking about spiritual things? Let your friendships be spiritual.

5. Be a public example of a godly friend. Others are always watching you, and your example could be used by God to encourage them. Don't ever forget that younger eyes are studying you and imitating your lifestyle.

The will of God can be a fearful thing if you don't know God. Many young adults think God's will is some scary, unknown fate—like waiting for a judge to hand down a prison sentence. But to a Christian who knows God, His will is a wonderful gift—like one you would receive on a birthday or Christmas morning.

As we close this chapter, we have another serious question: Do you trust God to make you happy? After all, God invented happiness! Nobody knows how to make you happy like God does. And the happiest place in life is in the center of His will.

So it's time to make a second choice—*choose to stay in God's will* right now, and tomorrow, and the next day. Choose God's will over every friend, every attraction, and every desire. Keep your friendships in His will. It is possible to be attracted to another person and to keep that developing relationship in the will of God.

Take a moment right now and ask God to help you stay in His will through your youth.

Personal Application

Think About It
Chapters 7–8

Assignment for Personal Application

Find a quiet place, a blank paper, and think through these practical exercises. Consider sharing this exercise with a parent, friend, a group of friends, or a teacher.

1. Describe what you believe is God's vision for your future.

2. When God brings the right person into your life, list the qualities that will matter most to you. List the qualities that should matter most to you. Are they the same list?

3. Describe why you believe God only reveals His will as we need to know it and only after we say "YES."

4. In what ways have you recently been struggling to stay in God's will? What will you do about those struggles?

5. If you had to prove in a court of law that your friendships are helping you to stay in God's will, what would you say?

Memorize this verse: "Without counsel purposes are disappointed: but in the multitude of counsellors they are established" (Proverbs 15:22).

Choose Controlled Emotions—Part 1

The third big choice you need to make to keep your relationships healthy is this: *choose to let God have complete and absolute control over your emotions.*

Have you ever seen a wildfire? We live in California, and our state is famous for them. In fact, just about every September, some part of California dominates the news because it is engulfed in flames. In recent years, large population areas like San Diego, Los Angeles, and San Francisco have been ravaged by fires that burn for days and even weeks.

Amazingly, investigators can always tell what started the fires. Sometimes it is something natural like lightning, or something unintentional like a spark from a campfire. Other times it is intentional. But one thing is consistent—a wildfire always starts small. A little spark combined with the right fuel and the right breeze can kick up a California wildfire in seconds.

Several years ago, I (Cary) witnessed a fire that began about a mile from our church in a field of brush. It was a windy day, and from my office window I watched a small fire become a large blaze that traveled a full mile to our church in just a few moments. It was scary and amazing at the same time!

Our church staff ran outside, grabbed garden hoses, and stood there realizing we were no match! Frankly, we looked like idiots. We didn't have the tools or the expertise to fight that fire!

Just before the flames leapt across the street to our church property, a large, well-equipped fire truck came roaring to the rescue. Firemen doused the flames with massive sprays of water—drenching all of us in the process. We didn't know what hit us!

When the smoke cleared, there we were, soaked and covered with soot, but alive and well. Our church was safe, and all we could do was cheer and give each other high-fives. Then we sheepishly wrapped up the garden hoses and thanked the firemen. I think they wanted to laugh at us.

Emotions between a guy and a girl are much like sparks. They can very quickly become blazes that rage out of control. And, don't take offense at this, but no young adult is equipped or ready to fight the blaze of raging emotions. It takes firefighters—God, parents, and spiritual authorities—to fight those kinds of fires. But the

Nine—Choose Controlled Emotions Part 1

best solution is to control the sparks so that they never turn into wildfires. It's best to control those emotions from the start—to make sure they don't become blazes.

You see, blazes do a lot of damage! Just like a wildfire can destroy lives, homes, and entire populations, even so, out-of-control emotions can destroy your heart and your future. First, let's talk about the fire and then we'll discover how to prevent it.

Emotions Out of Control

We mentioned earlier how a relationship develops. It takes two elements. Like a fire requires fuel and oxygen, so a relationship requires *time* and *attention*. The more time you spend with a person or the more attention you give a relationship when you're apart, the more emotions grow in that relationship. Someday this will be a normal and healthy part of your life.

We said it would be nice if we all had little gauges on our heads telling us when our emotions were getting too strong too early. Imagine if an alarm sounded and a little red light on your forehead began to flash every time you were getting too emotionally involved. How embarrassing would that be?! Isn't God good to spare you that feature?

Remember how we talked about your changing emotions? Well, one of the greatest dangers of boyfriend/girlfriend relationships is emotional dependency. This is also called *infatuation*. The word *infatuation* means "to be filled with an intense but short-lived passion or admiration for." The root meaning is "to be made foolish." The key words here are *intense*, *short-lived*, and *foolish*. *Intense* explains why these feelings are so overwhelming and real—especially to a young person. *Short-lived* explains why young adults experience so many "breakups"—in some circles it's almost like musical chairs! And *foolish* explains the condition of the mind when these emotions take over.

> One of the greatest dangers of youthful relationships is emotional dependency.

You must remember that the emotions you feel in a youthful guy/girl relationship are relatively new! Even if you've felt them before, your young heart isn't prepared to handle them well. Twitterpation is very powerful! It is intoxicating—like being emotionally drunk. Your reasoning becomes blurry. It's a good feeling, but it's also dangerous. Infatuation is like an illegal drug for your soul. It's an emotional high. You can't trust it, and you certainly can't build your life upon it.

Emotions are wonderful things—God created them and gave them to us. But they often lie. They were never meant to be trusted—just felt. They make wonderful feelings but terrible guides. God never, ever intended for you to be guided by emotion. Yet, in young attractions, they are usually setting the course—like rudders of a ship to young hearts. And usually emotions become the enemy because they grow too fast and burn out of

Nine—Choose Controlled Emotions Part 1

control. When they're done burning (and they soon will be), they always leave a lot of pain and regret.

Have you ever seen a large dog walking a small child? This is what emotions do to young hearts. No matter how strong you think you are, it's very easy to find yourself being dragged around by powerful, out-of-control feelings.

If you want to avoid this wildfire approach to friendships, then let's move on to the next chapter and find out what emotional dependency looks like.

TEN

Choose Controlled Emotions—Part 2

Signs of emotional dependency are easy to see—especially for your parents. They will be pointing this out to you earlier than you can see it. Be honest with yourself as you study these revealing points:

17 Signs of Emotional Dependency

When emotions start to burn too large, too fast, they leave telltale signs. This is what it looks like to be too emotionally involved in a friendship or a "crush":

1. Thinking about a person too much. You can't function at your best in school, church, or other life priorities because this person is always on your mind.

2. Getting jealous easily. Your friend can't relate with anyone else without you getting possessive.

3. Subconsciously expecting someone to be obligated to you. You take offense when your friend doesn't do what you expect them to do.

4. Needing to be in constant contact. You must call, email, text, talk constantly and without restraint. This is very dangerous and unhealthy.

5. Not having other friends. You lose touch with other good friendships because you are so consumed with one person.

6. Having to be alone with another person. You can't be with your friend in groups and still have a good time with the group.

7. Being easily offended at each other. You start misreading each other or having expectations that don't get met. This leads to endless, frivolous offenses and continual soap opera discussions—you know, the constant, "what's wrong—are you mad at me?" kind.

8. Saying I love you. This is always too soon in a teen relationship, and it always shows great immaturity when spoken too soon. Save this for the person to whom you will be engaged.

9. Starting to touch. It feels good, but needing to touch always means you are too emotionally involved.

10. Distancing from family. You can't enjoy being with your family because another person has essentially replaced those relationships.

Ten—Choose Controlled Emotions Part 2

11. Being irritable when apart. You're grumpy and hard to live with because your life is consumed with a boyfriend or girlfriend. This is your conscience troubling you because you are out of God's will.

12. Working out problems often. Long, emotional talks about "what's wrong" and trying to fix things become the norm.

13. Fear of losing that person. You can't imagine moving forward if this person stopped liking you. He or she completely defines your life.

14. Loss of interest in spiritual things. Your walk with God or your attention span in church suffers because you are consumed with another person.

15. Having to always be together. When you are at school, youth group, church or any other function, you *must* be with this person.

16. Giving your heart to another person. Someone other than God or your parents really has your heart.

17. Extreme despair during a breakup. You're nearly clinically depressed or suicidal because of a "breakup."

Now, if you read that list and think, "Oh my, that's my life!" Then welcome to the club—we were there once too! Don't be too hard on yourself. Every one of these feelings are intense. They are real and overwhelming. But if you don't do something fast, you risk the danger of emotions out of control—a blaze that could do serious damage.

Let's talk about how to rule emotions. What is God's solution for bringing these powerful forces into a safe zone?

How Emotions Can Be Controlled

Emotions need one thing—*restraint*. They must be told what to do and where to stay. Think about the two illustrations used earlier: A large dog needs a good collar, a leash, and a firm master. A fire needs a stone pit, a metal ring, a brick oven, or some sort of boundary. Even so, the only way to keep emotions from blazing out of control is to restrain them.

The good news is, God has given you several ways to control your emotions—ways to safely place them into a fireproof surrounding so they won't blaze. It's important for you to remember we're talking about *feelings*, so you're not going to *feel* like restraining your emotions. This is one area where *reason* must rule *romance*. Your emotions need a good leash and a firm Master. Your more serious, responsible, and sober side is going to have to *think* you into some decisions that don't *feel* very fun. But the product is burn free—so it's worth it. Part of God's command in Titus 2 is for you to learn to be *sober*—serious—being able to think your way into doing right.

Do you want to control your emotions? Then here's how:

Ten—Choose Controlled Emotions Part 2

1. Yield to God's Holy Spirit daily. Ephesians 5:18 says, "be filled with the Spirit." Get this: your emotions are often stronger than your will. In other words, your desires will be stronger than your ability to restrain them. You need more than your own strength. This takes a daily decision to give God control of your feelings. Ask the Holy Spirit throughout every day to strengthen you and control your emotions. Year after year you will grow stronger with God's help.

2. Ask for help. Restraining these emotions is over your head. You're dealing with big, nasty, powerful feelings. Without help, they will drag you around by the heart! You must ask your parents and others to help you—to tell you when they see emotions getting too strong and to put up boundaries to keep those emotions in check.

We're talking about specifics. Ask your parents to restrict how much time, how much contact, and how much attention you can give to a relationship. Your feelings will scream and resist those restraints, but your future spouse will thank you. Your emotions will HATE being restrained and everything in you will think your parents are too strict—but remember, these are only emotions talking. Reality is, you need help getting emotions under control.

3. Submit to the guidelines of your authorities. It's one thing to ask for restraint, it's another thing to obey the restraints. This is like giving up your garden hose and calling in the fire truck! For instance, when emotions are ablaze, it is extremely difficult to limit phone calls, emails, and text messages. It's very tough to sit with your family in church when someone you're interested in is sitting four rows away. It's miserable to go a week without being able to talk or spend time together. But again, these are powerful emotions, and that's why you need help restraining them. If it were up to you, they would blaze and burn unhindered, and you would burn out real soon. Follow your parents' guidelines—this is the fire pit that keeps the sparks from turning into a wildfire.

4. Make emotions follow truth. This one is the hardest. As you ask the Holy Spirit to control you, ask for help from your parents, and submit to authority, you will learn the art of letting emotions follow truth. In other words, you will learn to do what is right, regardless of how you feel. You will learn that feelings can change. Like a big dog can be trained, emotions can be reigned. Feelings can be forced to obey truth. The Bible calls this "ruling your spirit." Proverbs 16:32 says, "He that is slow to anger is better than the mighty; and he that ruleth his spirit than he that taketh a city." Again in Proverbs 25:28 God says, "He that hath no rule over his own spirit is like a city that is broken down, and without walls."

Did you catch that? Emotions uncontrolled make your life like a city without walls—no protection, no barriers. God desires for *you* to rule your *emotions*, not for your *emotions* to rule *you*. And frankly, there's no better training ground than in your guy/girl relationships in

Ten—Choose Controlled Emotions Part 2

which to learn how to rule your emotions. Learning to rule your emotions now will serve you well the rest of your life!

What to Do When Emotions Start to Grow

Because you are human, you *will* struggle with restraining emotions. Just prepare for it and expect it. When you begin to develop a healthy friendship with a guy or girl, this will be a major choice you will face every day. When you have discussions with godly parents about what is healthy and what isn't, you will sometimes disagree with them. Your heart will fight hard to have its way. And when you find yourself in the middle of a friendship and the Holy Spirit starts to warn you that your emotions are getting too strong, there are three simple things that you must do:

1. Spend less time together. Talk with your friend. Agree to keep the Lord first and to balance your time together. Decide to be comfortable hanging around other friends. Keep your relationship group-friendly—meaning, be able to have fun with the whole group, not just each other. Don't take every opportunity to be together. Say no sometimes, and if you aren't strong enough, let your parents say no for you.

Very early in many immature relationships a sense of *obligation* begins to develop. In other words, you feel like you *have to* do or be certain things for this person. Discuss this together and relieve each other of feeling obligated.

Don't be obligated to sit together, walk together, and constantly be together. Agree to be secure in your friendship and not possessive or manipulative of each other.

Limit your time together on purpose. Your age, your family life, and your parents' preferences are all factors in this equation. The less time you spend together, the less the flames of emotions will be able to burn.

2. **Give less attention to this relationship.** Have a life outside of one girl or one guy. When you are not together, don't be obsessed with each other. Limit your communication on purpose—less time on the phone (or none), fewer text messages (or none), fewer emails (or none), and less time thinking about, writing notes to, or generally investing your heart into this person. Honestly, during your young adult years it's not healthy to see the same person every day, then talk on the phone for hours, then email or social network multiple times, then text message until early morning. This only leads to a wildfire of emotion that you won't be able to control.

> God desires for you to rule your emotions, not for your emotions to rule you.

Try this on for size: one note per week, one email per week, one phone call per week, and limited time together. We've known many teens and college students who have conducted their relationships this way, and

Ten—Choose Controlled Emotions Part 2

it works! Many of them are very happily married today. They stayed in balance. Their hearts didn't burn out of control. Their friendships were not constant dramas. And through it all they learned the value of *controlled emotions*.

3. Be willing to take a break. Oh boy! This one is tough! When the time comes that emotions have a stranglehold on you, there's really only one thing to do—take a break. Stop communicating and spending time together. Stop giving attention to this relationship. It's like cutting off the oxygen and fuel supply for a fire. It's the toughest thing in the world, but over the years we have seen many young adults choose this path against the overwhelming power of screaming emotions. They are very wise and spiritually mature.

This isn't the same as a breakup. "Just friends" don't really break up. But sometimes a "just friends" relationship can become too close and too emotionally dependent. Your whole identity and security can be wrapped up into another person, and until you are close to marriage, this is never healthy.

Taking a break is like detox for your heart. It's like checking your emotions into rehab—you need the help of others and you'll feel like crying a lot. For a few weeks, your soul will go through withdrawals, and your heart will tell you that life is over. But over time, your heart will return to normal. The real you will return and everyone will know it. Sometimes this takes months, depending on how closely you walk with God.

We've seen young adults spare themselves a world of hurt because they realized their relationship was out of balance emotionally, and they chose to take a break. It's better if this decision is mutual, but it rarely is. It's a tough choice to make and even tougher to live with—but it has saved many lives from serious wildfires.

Do you remember the peach tree illustration? In a young tree you must pluck the early fruit and let the nutrients remain in the tree. This makes the tree stronger, healthier, and more fruitful over the long term.

Such is emotional strength. When you invest young emotions into infatuation, it's like wasting nutrients that you need. A right friendship will strengthen you, but unhealthy relationships drain you and make you weak. A wrong relationship cripples you and prevents the strong and fruitful adulthood that God intends for you.

When you experience attraction, you aren't doing anything wrong, but you are dealing with sparks. How will you handle those sparks? Will they jump out of the fire pit and become a wildfire? Will you try to fight the fire with a garden hose? Or will you call in the big trucks—parents and authorities?

The real problem with emotional attachment is that you're expecting someone to be the *strength* of your heart—and that's God's territory. No human can ever fill that place! Only God can be your strength—Psalm 73:26,

Ten—Choose Controlled Emotions Part 2

"My flesh and my heart faileth: but God is the strength of my heart, and my portion for ever."

Emotions *can be* restrained. It's time for you, by God's power, to "be the boss" of your emotions. You're mature enough to make the choice! It's time to stop letting emotions call the shots. Don't expect another person to be your stability. Look to God for strength, and let all emotions be governed by Him.

Think About It
Chapters 9–10

Assignment for Personal Application

Find a quiet place, a blank paper, and think through these practical exercises. Consider sharing this exercise with a parent, friend, a group of friends, or a teacher.

1. Have you experienced emotions of infatuation? Describe the experience.

2. List how many of the seventeen signs of emotional dependency you have personally experienced.

3. List the four steps to learning how to control emotions and make a commitment to start practicing them.

4. Is God convicting you that you are too emotionally involved right now? If so, describe what you should do about this situation.

5. Make a commitment to talk to someone in authority about your present or future relationships—write that person's name down. Then, write them a note explaining your commitment and asking for their help.

Memorize this verse: "My flesh and my heart faileth: but God is the strength of my heart, and my portion for ever" (Psalm 73:26).

ELEVEN

Choose Purity—Part 1

We never thought we would write this next paragraph to Christian young adults, but sadly, we must. We do so with heavy hearts—passionate to help you avoid the greatest mistake of many young lives.

You *will be* tempted to lose your purity during your young adult years. Someone, somewhere, at some point will try to get you to become sexually active in some way. Satan is already plotting how he will try to snare you sexually. To make matters worse, you live in a culture that is beyond obsession—it is delusional, destructive, and addictive about sexual activity.

Losing purity is a progression that begins with small steps and leads to great pain. And it comes with life-long consequences, so please read this chapter very carefully and respond with a firm commitment to purity.

Culture's Lies about Sex

Satan is out to rob you of the most precious thing you have outside of your soul—your purity.

Nearly 1,000,000 young women under age twenty become pregnant each year. That means close to 2,800 teens get pregnant each day. Not long ago a study was released showing that one in every four sexually active teenage girls in America has a sexually transmitted disease.

The world is constantly lying to you about sex. And many are buying the lies. Our culture promotes and encourages early sexual activity, abortion, homosexuality, pornography, and perversion of all types. Your world hammers you to lust, fantasize, and consume yourself with the flesh. But it's all lies! Every bit of it.

Culture teaches you to have sex safely. Be very clear—the only safe sex is between one man and one woman (husband and wife) who are committed to each other for life. This is God's recipe for the only fulfilling intimate relationship. Simply put—outside of marriage, a physical relationship doesn't fulfill, it destroys—it leaves you guilty, empty, confused, used, depressed, and frustrated. It promises love but delivers despair. It promises pleasure but returns pain. It promises fulfillment but leaves you wasted and wanting.

Believing culture's lies, modern families—even many Christians—are far off course on this subject. Sex-education classes in public schools combined with the

Eleven—Choose Purity Part 1

saturation of pornography and filth in our society has given many young people a twisted, perverted view of something wonderful that God created. Sadly, culture has introduced you to immorality and taught you to accept it as normal.

As a result, families are broken, lives are ruined, and divorce is at an all-time high. And never has the world had more suicidal, depressed, angry and confused young adults as a result of premarital sexual activity.

You are in a battle today, and the odds are against you. You are like a fish swimming upstream against a very strong current. It is difficult yet *very possible* to stay pure—but it won't happen by accident! If you are going to remain pure, which God commands, you must be *deliberate, intentional,* and *strategic*! You must choose purity on purpose because you value that wonderful someday that we already learned about.

Would you like to avoid the trap of immorality? Let's talk about it.

Getting the Right Information

In a world of lies, it's important that you get the right information about sex and purity. When a million voices are screaming lies at you, you must turn to the voices of truth.

Most young people get their information about sex from two places—*friends* and *media*. The problem is, friends have false information from media and bad experience. And media is constantly lying to you with sensational, entertaining stories—not truthful ones. So, friends and media are the wrong places to get information about sex.

There are only two right sources—two places you should go to learn about God's truth regarding the physical relationship between a man and a woman.

1. Go to God's Word. God has much to say about intimacy between a husband and wife, and it's all true! He is the Creator of this relationship, and He designed it for our blessing and benefit! Align your thinking with God's Word on this subject, and let Him be God. He places a high value on purity. Consider what God says in these verses about purity:

"Finally, brethren, whatsoever things are true, whatsoever things are honest, whatsoever things are just, whatsoever things are pure, whatsoever things are lovely, whatsoever things are of good report; if there be any virtue, and if there be any praise, think on these things" (Philippians 4:8).

"…keep thyself pure" (1 Timothy 5:22).

"Unto the pure all things are pure: but unto them that are defiled and unbelieving is nothing pure; but even their mind and conscience is defiled" (Titus 1:15).

"Let no man despise thy youth; but be thou an example of the believers, in word, in conversation, in charity, in spirit, in faith, in purity" (1 Timothy 4:12).

Eleven—Choose Purity Part 1

2. Go to parents or godly authorities. God expects you to hear the truth from those who desire the very best for you. Yet, for some reason, very few young adults and parents have a close enough relationship to talk about sex. This is a trap. The devil doesn't want you to have truthful answers from people who care. He would rather distance you from those people and have you misinformed.

You must get your parents to talk to you about this subject. Make them. Even if you're uncomfortable, make it happen. Take your questions, your curiosity, and your interests to your parents—they will give you straight answers and tell you the truth. There shouldn't be anything you can't talk about with them.

You can't afford to be told lies without having a reference point of truth. Knowing the truth makes you free to see the lies!

> You must choose purity on purpose because you value a wonderful someday.

If you don't have parents or if your parents do not believe God's Word on this matter, then find a godly, Bible-believing leader, preferably your gender, who can speak to you truthfully and cautiously. It is absolutely essential that you get truthful information from a godly person whom you can trust.

By the way—these conversations should be godly, holy, and respectful of the sacred subject, not giddy or light.

See Immorality as a Sin

God's Word clearly teaches that sex outside of marriage is wrong. This is more than a pointless rule—God doesn't create pointless rules. Every one of His laws is truthful and loving. They protect you and bless you with the best life. Every word of God is for your ultimate benefit! The verses below call immorality *fornication*—a word that simply means any kind of sexual sin:

"Flee fornication. Every sin that a man doeth is without the body; but he that committeth fornication sinneth against his own body" (1 Corinthians 6:18).

"But fornication, and all uncleanness, or covetousness, let it not be once named among you, as becometh saints;" (Ephesians 5:3).

"Nevertheless, to avoid fornication, let every man have his own wife, and let every woman have her own husband" (1 Corinthians 7:2).

"Mortify therefore your members which are upon the earth; fornication, uncleanness, inordinate affection, evil concupiscence, and covetousness, which is idolatry:" (Colossians 3:5).

"For this is the will of God, even your sanctification, that ye should abstain from fornication:" (1 Thessalonians 4:3).

"This I say then, Walk in the Spirit, and ye shall not fulfil the lust of the flesh" (Galatians 5:16).

"Dearly beloved, I beseech you as strangers and pilgrims, abstain from fleshly lusts, which war against the soul;" (1 Peter 2:11).

"But put ye on the Lord Jesus Christ, and make not provision for the flesh, to fulfil the lusts thereof" (Romans 13:14).

"And they that are Christ's have crucified the flesh with the affections and lusts" (Galatians 5:24).

Each of these verses make God's laws clear—sex outside of marriage is both wrong and dangerous. In the next chapter we're going to consider the consequences of breaking God's laws about sexual activity, and then we'll learn how to avoid this trap and stay pure.

TWELVE

Choose Purity—Part 2

God's Word says in Hebrews 11:25 that there is pleasure in sin for a season. But the reaping that follows immorality is unbearable. Sexual sin promises fun and pleasure, but it always delivers pain and problems. Staying pure before marriage is well worth it. Here's why:

Immorality Comes with a High Price Tag

Just like every sin, immorality has its consequences. The seeds eventually turn into a harvest. Immorality is the most personally devastating sin you could commit. The consequences are huge. Here are just a few of the high prices of premarital sexual activity:

1. **It robs you of your peace with God.** The sweetness, rest, joy, and comfort you once had is gone.

2. **It leaves you filled with guilt.** Your actions stay in your memory. They are never forgotten. And for the rest of your life, Satan will do his best to remind you and shame you.

3. **It breaks your fellowship with God** (Psalm 66:18). If ever there was a time you needed God, it is now. The sin of immorality breaks your close walk with Him.

4. **It hinders your usefulness for God.** God desires to use you for a great purpose, but He commands you to be a vessel fit for His use.

5. **It prevents the blessing of God.** Remember how David was chastened because of his sin with Bathsheba? One son rebelled and tried to kill him, one son raped his daughter, one son got killed, one son killed another son, and his baby died. All these were the consequences of one sin!

6. **It destroys you emotionally.** It brings shame, guilt, disappointment, and despair that weighs on your life like a mountain of granite. Your young heart and mind is not equipped to handle this, and your youth is too valuable to throw away.

7. **It destroys the relationship.** A relationship and the two lives in it are never the same after immorality.

8. **It robs your marital intimacy.** Every time you have a physical relationship outside of marriage, you are destroying your marriage before it even exists! Your

Twelve—Choose Purity Part 2

body belongs to God and a future spouse—don't ever give it to anyone else.

9. It risks disease. If a person will be immoral with you, the chances are that they have been with others before you.

10. It breaks trust. Being sexually active outside of marriage basically says, "You can't trust me inside of marriage." Physical intimacy prior to commitment instills distrust.

11. It leads others astray. Satan gets two for the price of one with this sin. Everything on this list happens in both people—each contributing to the fall of the other. On top of this, others are watching you, and someone like a younger sibling will likely follow you down the wrong path.

12. It risks pregnancy. Every child deserves to be born into a home where the mom and dad are married, in love, and committed for life. Every baby deserves to have parents that are old enough to provide. The hurt and pain of teen pregnancy is indescribable for the baby, the mom, and the family.

13. It leaves you disappointed and regretful. We counsel many people after immorality. Neither one of us has ever counseled someone who was really happy that they lost their purity. For reasons your parents should explain, you need to know that premarital sexual activity is disappointing, uncomfortable, and frustrating. The first time and the tenth time—every time, sex outside of marriage is never what God intended sex to be at all!

The aftermath is always guilt, pain, and regret. The tears and remorse last for years—while the relationship only lasted for moments. Trust us! Trust God. Immorality is just NOT WORTH IT!

14. It destroys the first experiences of your future marriage. Someday God will bring you together for the first time with a wonderful spouse. Don't ruin that awesome moment by giving it away for cheap and immediate disappointment!

There was once a father who would hammer a nail into a tree each time his son disobeyed. The son saw all the nails in the tree and was saddened by his actions. The father then agreed to remove a nail every time the son obeyed him. Eventually, the great day came when the father pulled the last nail out of the tree. The boy leaped for joy, but then began to cry when he noticed that, though the nails were removed, the scars still remained. The tree would never really be the same because the scars of his disobedience would still be there.

Though God can forgive and restore you from immorality, sadly, it places scars upon your life that will remain for a lifetime. How much better to stay pure and never place those scars upon your heart to begin with!

Avoiding Immorality

There are many influences in life that can lead you into immorality. If you desire to stay pure, we urge you to

Twelve—Choose Purity Part 2

avoid these traps—as every one of them can contribute, little by little, to your eventual fall:

1. Backsliding. Keep your heart soft, and walk closely and daily with God in His Word and prayer. Psalm 119:9, "Wherewithal shall a young man cleanse his way? by taking heed thereto according to thy word."

2. Rebellion. Trust your spiritual authorities. The truth is, the sexual relationship is a complex subject that you won't fully understand until many years into your marriage. Until then, don't rebel. Choose to trust and obey those who love you.

3. Sexual imagery. Guard your eyes! Whether online, at the mall, or at church—direct your eyes toward wholesome things and refuse to look at tempting or sexual images. There's a difference between seeing and looking. You can see something by accident and immediately look away. Looking is when you allow your eyes to linger or you choose to see.

4. Physical contact. Touching in a guy/girl relationship is never a good thing until you are married. We'll see why in the next chapter.

5. Emotional dependency. As discussed in the last chapter, emotional closeness always leads to physical closeness. This is God's design, but your young-adult years is the wrong time for emotional and physical closeness.

6. Clothing styles. Proverbs 6 and 7 speaks of the behavior of a wicked woman. Throughout God's Word we can see principles of modesty, appropriateness, and godliness when it comes to our dress. Be sure to wear clothing that contributes to holiness, modesty, and purity. We'll see this more closely later as well.

7. Time alone with a guy/girl. If you have a personal policy to never be alone with the opposite gender, then you're pretty much guaranteed to never lose your purity. What a great policy.

8. Lack of accountability. Another great policy is to never be "out of sight" of authority. Whether in another room or another car—a lack of accountability always brings increased temptation.

9. Impure imagination. Immorality always starts in the mind. Satan will attack your mind first. Therefore you must guard the gates to your mind—your eyes and your ears. Psalm 101:3 says, "I will set no wicked thing before mine eyes…." What you see and hear become thoughts, attitude, desires, and eventually *actions*. Fill your mind with God's Word, godly music, and biblical principles.

Thinking wrongfully about sex will lead you to experiment. Seek God's help to direct your thoughts into His Word and away from sexual thinking. God commands us in 2 Corinthians 10:5 to bring every thought into captivity to the obedience of Christ. This requires a daily commitment to fill our minds with good things.

10. Corrupt communication. Guard your life from the world's music, cursing, and dirty jokes. Guard your heart from filthy TV shows and

Twelve—Choose Purity Part 2

movies. "Evil communications corrupt good manners" (1 Corinthians 15:33).

The tongue is always a reflection of the heart. The Bible teaches us in James 3 that if we control our tongues we can direct our whole lives—like the rudder of a ship or the bridle of a horse. Your communication not only reveals your heart, it also directs your heart. If you choose not to talk or communicate suggestively, you are protecting your purity.

11. Peer pressure. Many Christians fall morally because "everyone else is doing it." Stand strong in the Lord and choose to remain pure, no matter what everyone else is doing.

12. Sinful media. Music, movies, TV, romance novels, internet, pornography, social networking—the list could go on. The devil will do anything he can to gain a foothold in your heart. Rather than try to list all of the weapons that Satan could invent, God addressed it quite simply when He said, "Keep thy heart with all diligence; for out of it are the issues of life" (Proverbs 4:23). Lock up the doors of your heart, and refuse to allow any impurity!

13. Desire to prove something. Many young adults become sexually active trying to prove themselves in some way. Guys desire to prove their manliness while girls desire to prove that they are attractive to someone. Find your security in the Lord so that you have nothing to prove.

14. Misunderstanding of love. Sex is not love. In marriage, sex can be an expression of love, but only one of many. Before marriage, true love always does what is best for the other person. Therefore, in your guy/girl relationships, true love will always protect purity.

15. Curiosity. There's nothing wrong with needing answers about this topic. Every young person is curious about this matter. The problem is in *where* you take that curiosity. Take it to God and your parents or another godly leader.

We've just seen fifteen things that lead to immorality and how to avoid them. If you value your purity, you will have to fight for it.

Proverbs 30:12 says, "There is a generation that are pure in their own eyes, and yet is not washed from their filthiness." There is very little reverence for purity in this generation. Young lady, that young man who wants you to be impure will never be a good husband. If he cannot control himself now, he will never be faithful to you. Young man, that young lady belongs to the Lord and her father—if she will give herself away prematurely, she will never make a good wife.

Decide now that you will fight for purity—that you will stand guard over your purity. One day your spouse will thank you!

> Decide now that you will fight for purity. One day your spouse will thank you!

Twelve—Choose Purity Part 2

Recovering from Past Failure

If you have read this chapter thinking, "I've already lost my purity," then we have a few words for you. Yes, you made mistakes. Yes, there are consequences. Yes, you will always regret those decisions. But God still has a plan for you. God loves you, and His grace can help you. His mercy can cleanse you and place you on a pathway of hope and blessing.

Though you will always have the scars and regret, deal biblically with your past and make the right decisions for your future. You should decide to be pure from this day forward. Here's how to recover from those bad decisions:

1. Confess the sin to God if you have not already done so. Read 1 John 1:9 and Psalm 51.

2. Learn from your past sin. Stop and figure out what led to your immorality. What were your mistakes? Think this through so you don't repeat the process.

3. Apologize to the person who was involved. Don't blame the other person, but rather forgive. Take responsibility, make the conversation short, and tell this person you are sorry for the sin.

4. Tell your parents, pastor and/or counselor. Go to parents and spiritual leaders who can help to restore you.

5. Put it behind you, and do not bring it up again. Don't discuss your mistakes with other friends. This is not appropriate conversation.

6. Do not dwell on it (Philippians 4:8). Do not allow your mind to dwell on this sin. Do what the Apostle Paul did—forget those things which are behind.

7. Cleanse your heart in God's Word. Nothing can purify a mind and heart like God's Word. Immorality in the life of a Christian always starts by neglecting the Bible. Young adults who spend much time in the Word of God are stronger against temptation.

I (Mike) taught a lesson along these lines once to our youth group and passed a white rose around the room for everyone to touch and feel the petals. Afterwards, no one thought the rose looked all that different, until I took out another white rose—this one completely untouched. The touched rose had lost much of its beautiful color!

No godly person desires to marry a person who has been passed around to many partners! Your purity is like a precious flower—and a lot of people would like to snatch it away. Don't let that happen! Save it. Hold it tight. And on your wedding day give it away to the one for whom it was intended.

I (Mike) will never forget seeing the famous "Hope Diamond" in the Smithsonian Institute in Washington, D.C. They said it was "priceless." It was sealed in a glass case, in a brick wall with a burglar alarm and an armed guard. I thought, "I wish young Christians would guard their purity this much." Surely purity is much more valuable than that diamond!

Twelve—Choose Purity Part 2

Have you ever made a promise to God to keep yourself pure? If not, why not make Him that promise today? Why not pray sincerely right now and vow to be pure? If you have done that already, put the date (approximate) here.

Date: _____

Signed: _____

The Product of Purity

Do you want a great husband or wife someday? Do you want a fantastic, out-of-this-world marriage? Do you want to enjoy a wonderful, physical relationship for the rest of your life? These things all flow from purity! The path to wonderful, physical intimacy begins with purity.

One day your fiancé may ask you if you are a virgin. Think about that moment. Decide now that you will be able to answer, "YES!" One day your children may ask you about purity. Be able to tell them that purity was worth the wait!

The product of purity is worth all the waiting, all the fighting, all the enduring. Temptation can be strong, especially when you are growing close to someone who you believe you love. But by staying pure and resisting temptation, you are building strength into your life. You are discovering how to be

> The product of purity is worth all the waiting, all the fighting, all the enduring.

faithful, how to be committed, and how to be selfless. You are learning to say no to the flesh. That strength will one day pay off with a faithful, committed, and selfless marriage. In that relationship you will greatly enjoy the spiritual and physical intimacy in the way that God originally designed. And that's worth the wait!

As an end note to this chapter: there are many perverted forms of sexual activity that are prevalent today. Homosexuality, incest, and sexual abuse abound in our society. If you have been involved in any of these unbiblical and hurtful things, we would urge you to get pastoral and biblical counseling to find God's grace for healing, restoration, and recovery.

This has been a very serious chapter, and the next one is the same. You may need to take a break, think about these things, and seriously covenant with God that you will value what He values—choose purity!

Twelve—Choose Purity Part 2

Think About It
Chapters 11–12

Assignment for Personal Application

Find a quiet place, a blank paper, and think through these practical exercises. Consider sharing this exercise with a parent, friend, a group of friends, or a teacher.

1. Describe any ways you have sensed temptation pulling you toward impurity.

2. Describe where your information about sex, up to this point, has come from. Make a commitment to go to God and parents or spiritual authority.

3. Write out three of the five verses listed at the end of chapter 11.

4. Make your own list—what would happen in your life if you lost your purity? What would it cost you? Take your time and make the list as long as you can. Save this list and read it once a week until you get married.

5. Of the fourteen things that lead toward immorality, write out the specific ones that God convicted you of. Next to each one, describe how will you respond to each.

6. Write one or two paragraphs describing what will happen in your life if you will stay pure until you get married.

Memorize this verse: "But put ye on the Lord Jesus Christ, and make not provision for the flesh, to fulfil the lusts thereof" (Romans 13:14).

THIRTEEN

Choose "No Touch"—Part 1

There is a story of a camel who was resting outside of his master's tent one cold night. He became so cold that he finally asked his master if he could stick the very tip of his nose inside the tent just to warm it up. Reluctantly, his master agreed. After a few moments, his nose was so warm and felt so good that he asked if he could put his front paws in the tent as well. Again the master agreed. Not long after, the master drifted off to sleep, and gradually the camel slipped his hump and then finally his back legs into the tent. By the time the morning arrived, the master awakened to find himself sleeping in the cold outdoors—having been completely nudged out by his camel.

A physical relationship between a guy and a girl is the same way. If you give an inch, it will take a mile. The most common first step into immorality is when two young people decide to start touching.

We are often asked, "Is it okay for guys and girls to touch in any way? Can we hold hands? Can we give a good-night kiss? Can we put our arms around each other? What about just sitting close?" These are good questions from sincere hearts. Many sincere and spiritual people are snagged on these seemingly innocent points because of things they don't understand. And so we'd like to give you some solid principles to help you understand this matter.

If you want your guy/girl relationships to stay healthy and helpful, you will have to make this big choice—*don't touch each other*. Now before you rule us out as being extreme, please read this chapter with an open heart. We believe the Bible and good logic will help you come to the same conclusion we have.

Physical Affection Is Good

First, it's important for you to know that physical affection and a loving touch is essentially a good thing. God created these expressions of love, but like all of God's creations, they have boundaries—God's design and intended use. Physical kinds of love have *appropriate* and *inappropriate* expressions.

For instance, every child needs physical affection from parents and loving family members. Every spouse needs physical affection and love from a husband or wife.

Thirteen—Choose "No Touch" Part 1

Someday in your future, physical affection between you and the one you have committed your life to should be a wonderful and abundant thing! At the right time, the right place, and with the right person you can one day pour out all of your hugs, kisses, and snuggles without limits—no need to hide it, break rules, or fear getting caught. It will all be appropriate and godly at that time.

Until then, God has other plans. Let's discover them.

God's Short-Term Goal

While God's *long-term* goal for your life is the abundant fulfillment of the physical desires He created, He has a different *short-term* goal to protect your long-term happiness.

Have you ever seen a building under construction? Long before walls, floors, ceilings, paint, carpet, or furniture is put into place, there is a foundation. No one goes to an empty lot and starts building walls and placing furniture randomly. There's a process to building a structure, and the foundation always comes first. If the foundation is solid and stable, then your options for walls, furniture, and decor are endless.

Have you ever seen a really nice birthday cake—one with really great decorations? What if you went to cut into that cake only to find a cardboard box underneath the icing? Not only would you be disappointed, the "cake" would be useless.

Such is a physical relationship prior to marital commitment. It can appear sweet, but it's actually empty, shallow, meaningless, and weak. It's like a building with no foundation—it's destined to fall down. It's like decorating a cake box.

Right now God is building a foundation, and being physical with a guy or girl only takes away from what He is building; it doesn't contribute! The physical is the decoration of a great love that you will someday experience. But even then, it's only the decoration—it's never the sole substance. Someday when you are married, the physical part of marriage will be a *very important* part of your relationship, but it will also be a *relatively small* part of your total relationship. Being physical never held a marriage together. Being physical is the expression of what holds a marriage together.

> Being physical never held a marriage together. Being physical is the expression of what holds a marriage together.

In marriage, commitment and character are like the steel girders of a skyscraper—what all the walls and finishings hold on to. The physical act of marriage is supposed to be supported by the steel structure of commitment and integrity. Think of it this way—you will never want to kiss a person who won't take care of you, stay faithful to you, or build a strong life with you. Being physical as a young person is an attempt to place the decorations in place before the foundation is built.

Thirteen—Choose "No Touch" Part 1

What is God building in you right now? He's building the foundation and the steel structure—self-control, commitment, and integrity. He's building self-discipline and strength. But if you give in to your physical desires, you cheat yourself of that growth and weaken your future.

When we were your age, a question we both wondered was: Why does God allow physical desires to awaken at thirteen only to tell me that I must wait to fulfill them? It doesn't seem fair! Why wouldn't God wait to awaken those desires until close to marriage?

The answer is simple. God is building something very valuable in you—the power of "no." He's helping you to establish the ability to control and direct those desires before you get married.

God's Word says in 1 Corinthians 9:27, "But I keep under my body, and bring it into subjection: lest that by any means, when I have preached to others, I myself should be a castaway."

Earlier He says in 1 Corinthians 9:25, "And every man that striveth for the mastery is temperate in all things. Now they do it to obtain a corruptible crown; but we an incorruptible." God wants to be the master of your body, and He wants you to have control of your desires.

You see, restraining your physical desires before marriage is the best proof that you can keep them in bounds after marriage. So, in not being physical now, you are learning patience and temperance for the rest of your life.

The Power of Physical Touch

Have you ever seen a dam? In central California there is a large reservoir that feeds into a massive structure for generating electricity and watering the central valley of California.

The power of water is a good power. Water can create electricity, provide nutrients to crops, and sustain humanity. Water is a great thing.

> Restraining your physical desires before marriage is the best proof that you can keep them in bounds after marriage.

A dam and reservoir are good things as well. Why? Because they *restrain* the power of the water. They hold back that power until the right time, and then carefully direct the right amount and the right flow of water to the right place so good things can happen.

Imagine if we climbed up that dam with a pickax and started whacking away until we finally created a crack in the dam. What would happen?

Nothing at first. But soon a tiny trickle of water would start to flow. Initially it might not hurt anything, but that tiny trickle doesn't belong there. And it has a power that is subtle and relatively unseen—it's going to become a much bigger problem. Over time, that trickle

Thirteen—Choose "No Touch" Part 1

would force the crack to widen. Soon the widened crack will begin to break away, and eventually a large body of water will come crashing through the dam and down upon civilization—destroying anything in its path.

The power of *unrestrained* water is bad! But the power of *restrained* water is good. Even so, the power of restrained physical desires is good, and the power of unrestrained physical desires is bad.

Your physical desires are like that water. One day they will be directed into the right relationship at the right time to create wonderful love and life. Like the water, those physical desires will put nutrients and strength into your relationship.

Right now, God is building the dam in your life. He's teaching you how to say "no" to those desires—how to keep them where they belong. He wants those physical expressions to be held back in reserve—like a reservoir. He wants you to learn the power of restraint. For in restraining desires, you're saving them for the right person at the right time. And you're learning how to control that awesome power once you finally begin to use it in marriage.

Just like the water creates healthy crops and energy—even so, you must learn how to manage and direct the power of your physical desires. You must grow in understanding how to use them for good and prevent them from crashing down upon your life.

Being physical in a young relationship is like creating a tiny little crack in the wall of your dam. You might think it's fine and nothing worse is going to happen, but you are wrong. Your body was not designed to allow tiny cracks of physical activity before marriage. They always widen and lead to destruction.

Now is the time to restrain—to train those desires when and where they are allowed to flow.

In a world where most young adults don't understand these principles, you will have a giant head start if you will deeply consider what we're studying. In the next chapter we will look more closely at the power of physical touch and why a "no touch" policy is the best policy.

FOURTEEN

Choose "No Touch"—Part 2

The choice not to touch is a difficult one—especially in today's culture. It's not uncommon to see even junior highers in public places with their hands all over each other. This is one area where peer pressure is massive, and cultural trends are definitely working against you! But we believe you can see the truth and be wiser than most young people. Let's look closer at why touching is a losing proposition for guy/girl friendships.

Why Many Marriages Fail

Do you know why so many marriages fail? Because many young people never learned how to restrain this amazing power. *Divorces are made of grown-up teenagers who never learned about restraint.* After the wedding day, rather than finding fulfillment in marriage, their unrestrained desires spilled over, leaked out, and broke out into affairs and other forms of immorality. The power that they didn't restrain as teens, they also didn't restrain as adults.

Think about the illustration of the water and the dam as you read this verse: "But every man is tempted, when he is drawn away of his own lust, and enticed. Then when lust hath conceived, it bringeth forth sin: and sin, when it is finished, bringeth forth death" (James 1:14-15). Do you see the *trickle* effect? Little by little, temptation wears away the cracks and finally the whole dam comes crashing down.

> Divorces are made of grown-up teenagers who never learned about restraint.

Good marriages fail because young people never learned the principle of the reservoir. They never learned restraint. The Bible uses many words for restraint—like flee, abstain, mortify—but it says one primary thing: avoid lust and immorality like the plague! Think about God's words to you in these verses:

"Flee also youthful lusts: but follow righteousness, faith, charity, peace, with them that call on the Lord out of a pure heart" (2 Timothy 2:22).

"Dearly beloved, I beseech you as strangers and pilgrims, abstain from fleshly lusts, which war against the soul;" (1 Peter 2:11).

Fourteen—Choose "No Touch" Part 2

"Mortify therefore your members which are upon the earth…" (Colossians 3:5).

At the very least, being physical with a guy or girl makes "provision for the flesh"—which we are specifically commanded not to do. "But put ye on the Lord Jesus Christ, and make not provision for the flesh, to fulfil the lusts thereof" (Romans 13:14). Making provision for the flesh is like allowing a crack in the dam. It is giving place to temptation.

Perhaps you've heard the story of the little boy who was told by his father not to swim in the pool near his house. An hour later, the father found the boy near the pool with his swimsuit on. When asked why he had his swimsuit on, the boy replied, "Just in case I get tempted." The boy gave place to the flesh—he was actually inviting temptation rather than protecting himself.

Even so, when you start touching "just a little" you are inviting greater temptation, and you won't be strong enough to resist.

God's Word says that "little sins" don't stay little—a little leaven messes up the whole lump! A little folly messes up the whole life. Ecclesiastes 10:1 says, "Dead flies cause the ointment of the apothecary to send forth a stinking savour: so doth a little folly him that is in reputation for wisdom and honour."

Even so, a little touching becomes a big problem and can lead to seriously damaging your life, your testimony, and your future. God makes this principle very clear in 1 Corinthians 7:1, "Now concerning the things whereof ye wrote unto me: It is good for a man not to touch a woman."

The Biological Progression

Getting touchy in a guy/girl relationship is a step in the wrong direction—and once you take that step it leads to other wrong choices. It becomes a downward slide that doesn't correct itself and is very difficult to reverse. Why is this?

God designed physical affection to be expressed in two contexts. The first is what we might call *friendly* or *loving affection*. This is what is expressed from parents to children, between siblings, or even good friends—like a hug or a pat on the back. Between a guy and a girl who are interested in each other, this is usually the initial intent, but friendly affection is really an impossibility in a guy/girl relationship. We'll see why in a moment.

The second kind of affection would be considered *sexual affection*—the kind of touching designed to end in physical intimacy. For the sake of appropriateness, let's just say that God designed your biological responses very specifically. Your senses and your emotions can be heightened sexually and can become active easily. All it takes is the right kind of touch from someone you find attractive.

Frankly, this is why touching is so much fun—because your body is responding and it just feels right and good. But this is also why it is dangerous. Your body,

Fourteen—Choose "No Touch" Part 2

when awakened sexually, starts a progression—it starts with holding hands and light touching, moves to kissing and making out, and is designed to end with physical intimacy. This is God's good creation to be experienced in marriage.

In a guy/girl relationship, touching just isn't friendly affection, no matter what you tell yourself. It's impossible. Your brain and body are not designed that way. Holding hands, hugging, and kissing between a guy and girl are simply the first steps of the biological progression of sexual desire. If you don't want to be immoral, don't start the biological progression. It's just that simple.

A Double Dead End Road

Starting to be physical places your friendship on a road with two dead ends. It suddenly has no place to go. Few young adults know about this, so read carefully.

The moment you start to hold hands or touch in other ways, you are signaling the soon coming and frustrating end of your friendship. Let's explain.

When you start getting physical, you start the biological progression. Which means, you either have to *finish it* or *stop it*. There are no other options. And if you are committed to purity, finishing it is not an option, which means you must decide where to stop.

There's nothing more frustrating between a guy and a girl than starting the physical progression and then trying to stop it. Many young adults tell themselves that this is possible, but they have no clue how overpowering this progression is. For instance, they decide they will only hold hands or sit close. Or they decide to only kiss goodnight once and then they will stop.

Have you ever seen young relationships where both the guy and the girl are like well-shaken, two-liter bottles of soda—ready to explode in frustration? The joy, the happiness, and the lightness is gone. Suddenly the relationship is like a five-hundred-pound weight dragging both people down into discouragement and anxiety. This is the result of touching and trying to stop! It's the worst! And it just doesn't work.

> Good marriages fail because young people never learned the principle of the reservoir. They never learned restraint.

Once the physical has begun, we either give in to sexual temptation and destroy ourselves, or we try to stop the progression—which we aren't designed to do. The progression isn't supposed to stop. It's like lighting a firecracker then hoping it won't go off. Therefore trying to stop is *nearly impossible*, and when we stop, the heart and body become very frustrated!

The point is, when you start touching, you have no place to go! You can't lose purity, and you can't wrestle with the constant pressure of unfulfilled desires. Eventually your friendship will explode—either in failure or in frustration. Touching is truly the beginning of a double dead end.

Fourteen—Choose "No Touch" Part 2

The Heart Connection

One last thought on the "touching" subject. Guys are primarily physical—they like to look at and touch girls for physical pleasure. While girls are primarily emotional—they like to feel loved in their hearts. For a guy, touching is primarily a physical act. But for a girl, touching is an emotional act. It involves the heart—BIG TIME!

Young man, if you touch a young lady, you think she's experiencing the same surface pleasure that you are. Not so. She's investing her heart! The problem is that you don't own her heart or her body. Only God and her father should have possession of that heart until she is close to marriage. Keeping your hands off of a young lady shows great respect for her heart, her father, her God, and her future husband (even if it is you!).

Young lady, this is one great reason not to let a young man touch you. It doesn't have the same meaning for him that it has for you. No young man deserves your heart until later. Unless a guy is committing himself to you at a wedding altar, physical activity isn't love, it's just physical pleasure. You think his heart is invested. He may even tell you it is. But be sure, a guy who will take advantage of your body before marriage does not love you. He is, at best, immature and ignorant of what's really going on. And besides that, he can't control himself, which means he won't make a very good husband unless something changes. He needs to stop touching you and focus on learning self-control.

Don't give your heart to a guy by being physical. Don't endear the heart of a young lady by touching her. Decide to restrain out of respect for your God and your future spouse.

It's time to make a choice. If you're involved in a seriously touchy relationship you should walk away. Yes. Break it off—as soon as possible. If you've just started touching, talk to your parents and get their counsel. Perhaps, with their help, you could bring your friendship back into the bounds of safety and decide to stop touching.

> Restrain your physical desires out of respect for your God and your future spouse.

It's best, early in your relationship, to talk to your friend and agree together not to touch. This is the easiest and most rewarding path—but it's also the toughest, so be prepared to battle your flesh.

If you are ever in a situation where touching begins, walk away quickly—flee—and find better friends.

Do you live your Christian life seeing how close you can get to sin without getting hurt? Or do you live staying as far from sin as possible? Those who live close to the lines always experiment with crossing the lines. Then, after they are comfortable crossing the lines, they cross more often. It's only a matter of time before they get hit by a truck, and then in desperation wonder how to fix the mess they've created. If you want to keep

Fourteen—Choose "No Touch" Part 2

from crossing God's lines, stay as far away from them as possible.

If you want the best youth, the healthiest friendships, and the most mature approach for marriage and a great future—choose "no touch"! God's will for your life does not include touching yet. The biological progression cannot be completed.

Right now God desires to strengthen your ability to say "no." He intends to build your reservoir, store up your desires, and then release them within the commitment of marriage where they will bring abundant life, joy, closeness, and intimacy.

Once again, it's all about the right person at the right time. And until then, it's about becoming the right person. Saving your body and guarding your heart now makes you a much better spouse later.

As we close this chapter, think of this: when you keep your hands off of your friend, you can have a clear conscience with God, with your parents, with your friend's parents, and with all others. Dr. Paul Chappell often says, "There's no softer pillow than a clear conscience."

There's something mighty powerful about living with nothing to hide!

Think About It
Chapters 13–14

Assignment for Personal Application

Find a quiet place, a blank paper, and think through these practical exercises. Consider sharing this exercise with a parent, friend, a group of friends, or a teacher.

1. Describe in your own words God's short-term goal for our physical desires.

2. In relation to premarital physical activity in relationships, explain, in your own words, why many marriages fail.

3. Write out three of the verses from chapter 14.

4. Have you ever experienced a relationship that was on the double dead end road? Describe what happened to the relationship.

5. List five to ten reasons, in your own words, why you believe it's best not to touch each other in a guy/girl friendship.

Memorize these verses: "But I keep under my body, and bring it into subjection: lest that by any means, when I have preached to others, I myself should be a castaway" (1 Corinthians 9:27).

"And every man that striveth for the mastery is temperate in all things. Now they do it to obtain a corruptible crown; but we an incorruptible" (1 Corinthians 9:25).

FIFTEEN

Choose Family First

During my (Cary) ninth grade year, my dad briefly took a new job that became a strain on his schedule and prevented us from having a lot of time together. As I look back, I'm amazed how the devil tried to weaken our relationship during this very important time.

Fortunately, my dad and mom were sensitive to the needs of our family and didn't relegate my spiritual training to the church, the youth group, or the Christian school (though we were active in all three).

When it came to a choice between keeping our family strong or making the new job work, my parents chose family first. I'll never forget the night they sat us all down to explain that we would be moving across the country to a new job that would give us more family time. That move took us to California and gave way

Just Friends

to untold divine appointments in my life and future—including meeting my future wife in tenth grade! Yet, in the short term, it was an incredibly difficult thing for my brothers and me to accept. We had to leave our friends and our lives back East and start new ones on the West Coast. That's a tall order for three guys younger than fifteen.

I'm thankful that my parents were willing to move heaven and earth to maintain our family time—our connection. Far more than I needed my sports, my friends, or my "life"—I needed Dad and Mom, and they went to great lengths to protect "us"!

> When you establish a relationship of honor with your mom and dad, you place yourself directly in the path of God's blessings.

Why didn't I run to rebellion, sex, drugs, alcohol, or other forms of "pain-killers" when I was a teen? I simply didn't need to. I had Dad and Mom, and we were really good friends. My heart was strong because my relationships at home were strong. That's how God intended it to be.

Psalm 73:26 says, "My flesh and my heart faileth: but God is the strength of my heart, and my portion for ever." God wants your heart to be strong. He wants you to find your spiritual and emotional stability in His plan. And for now, a large part of that stability and strength will come from a good relationship with your family.

Fifteen—Choose Family First

And so we come to the next big choice you must make to keep your guy/girl friendships healthy and helpful—*choose family first*! Choose to have strong and honoring relationships with your parents, and choose to be friends with your siblings while you still can.

Lost in Your Own Home

Recent studies show that the average teen spends less than a few minutes per day with parents. For many it is normal to avoid parents altogether—to spend countless hours locked up in a room or to stay out with friends as much as is humanly possible. In these cases, friends become the de facto family—they essentially replace the role of your parents and siblings, but they can never provide the strength that God intends to give your heart.

When it comes to guy/girl relationships, bad ones are always linked to a weak heart that has lost its connections at home. The best defense against youthful temptations is a close relationship with Mom and Dad! No wonder the devil fights this relationship so hard during your teen years. Young people who are relationally distant from parents are highly vulnerable and easily led astray by wrong influences. Those who are close to their parents have strong hearts—able to stand against temptation!

God makes a very important promise in Ephesians 6:2–3, "Honour thy father and mother; which is the first commandment with promise; That it may be well with thee, and thou mayest live long on the earth."

When you establish a relationship of honor with your mom and dad, you place yourself directly in the path of God's blessings.

It is possible, during your youth, to feel lost in your own home—like a stranger that nobody really knows. But it's up to you to prevent this. Here's why:

Your Home Will Follow You

In the book of Genesis, God tells the story of elderly Isaac (almost blind) desiring to bless his oldest son before his death. The "blessing" was symbolic of approval and God's blessing upon the eldest son. It was like the baton of faith and affirmation being handed off. Esau was the oldest son and deserved the blessing. However, his younger brother, Jacob, disguised himself and stole the blessing. Esau hated Jacob after that and sought to kill him.

Just as Jacob desired the blessing of his father, you do too. Your heart craves the affirmation and acceptance that only your parents can provide. It's why you panicked when you got lost in the grocery store as a little kid. It's why you didn't want to stay home alone when you were younger. We all draw strength and identity from our parental relationships.

More importantly, the relationships we have at home will follow us for the rest of our lives. We establish habits and patterns of relating to others. These habits filter into our future in untold thousands of little ways.

Fifteen—Choose Family First

God has given most people eighteen or twenty years at home—give or take some, depending upon God's will. During those years we face a million different social and life situations. We learn how to interact, to love, to resolve conflict, and to grow up. We learn how to respond to the strengths and weaknesses of others. We basically learn all of the people skills that will follow us for the rest of our lives. Your walk with God and your family relationships are the most important part of the equation. More than you realize, your home is the testing and training ground of your future.

With this in mind, here are a few important things to consider:

1. Satan is attacking the home. Satan doesn't want you to be right with your parents. That must mean this relationship is very important. If Satan attacks it, then you should fight for it.

2. Bible characters had rough home situations too. Joseph was sold into slavery by his brothers. Esau had his birthright stolen by his brother. Hagar and Ishmael were kicked out of Abraham's house. Jephthah had a harlot for a mother. No one has a perfect home, but every home is a learning environment—so have a soft heart regardless of your home situation.

Rough home situations are not new. If you have a broken or struggling home, God desires to use it for your good in some way. Your parents and family are tools God uses to mold your life.

3. How you treat your parents will be how you treat your spouse. You are becoming what you will be. Your life's patterns are being engraved upon your heart. If you are hateful, rude, selfish, rebellious, proud, irreverent, deceitful, or disrespectful now, you will be in the future—unless you change soon! Ask yourself the following questions concerning your family members:

> Do I love my parents and show it?
> Am I considerate?
> Am I gone too much?
> Do I argue with them?
> Do I act immature? (tantrums, pouting)
> Do I say things I don't mean? ("I hate you")
> Do I obey instantly with a good spirit?
> Do I try to see my parents' perspective?
> Do I pray for my parents and family?
> Is my heart right toward my family?

If you would like to become the right person, most of your work is "home work." Young lady, you will one day set the atmosphere of your home (Titus 2:5), and your relationship with your husband will in many ways mirror your relationship with your father. Young man, you will be the leader of your home, and you will most likely treat your wife very similarly to how you treat your mother. What a huge responsibility and challenge! If you want a great wife, find a young lady that treats her father well. If you want a great husband, find one that is respectful and loving towards his mother.

Fifteen—Choose Family First

4. Future family relationships will mirror sibling relationships. Most young people give very little attention to being a good brother or sister. But several Bible characters were really good examples: Andrew and Peter; James and John; Mary, Martha, and Lazarus. Nowhere does the Bible say Christian brothers and sisters have a right to argue, bicker, and fight incessantly. Psalm 133:1 says, "Behold, how good and how pleasant it is for brethren to dwell together in unity!"

If you can build a great relationship with your brothers or sisters, you're going a long way in spiritual growth and preparation for your future. Ask God to help you do the following toward your siblings:

Desire for them to be spiritual.
> (Andrew wanted Peter saved.)

Encourage them.
> (They go through some tough times, too.)

Speak well of them.

Love them in word and action.

Pray daily for them.
> (It is hard to argue with someone you pray for.)

Don't tell their faults to others.

Be sensitive to their needs.
> (Help them get through struggles.)

Be a peacemaker in arguments.

Don't take them for granted.
> (They won't always be there.)

Treat them as well as you treat other friends.

What if I Don't Have a Father?

What if you don't know who your father is or he is absent from your life? What if your parents are divorced and your home is already a wreck? Well, first know that this is huge. No one deserves to experience this, and the pain and burden you carry is extreme—probably more than you even realize.

Primarily this means you are more vulnerable, and you must take careful steps to protect and prepare yourself. You must choose God's grace and look to Him for daily strength to forgive and move forward. We both have watched many young people grow up in broken homes. We've seen many destroy themselves out of anger and bitterness toward family. Yet we've seen many defy the odds, claim God's grace, and grow up to live God's best! They decided not to let the mistakes or wounds from a previous generation rob them of their own "wonderful someday!"

You too can defy the odds! Someone else's decisions don't have to ruin your life. So what can you do? You'll have to realize that God is your Father. Spend extra time in His Word so you know what He's saying. If you'll read Luke 15 slowly, you'll find He has all the character traits you need. He is good and loving. He desires a relationship with you. He is available for communication. He gives a lot of freedom. He is faithful and always there for you. He is merciful. He looks for your return when you are

Fifteen—Choose Family First

distanced from Him. He is generous, and He loves you like you are His only child!

First Things First

God always blesses right priorities. If you have close friends that you respect, honor, and cherish while at the same time your relationships at home are fragmented, strained, harsh, and disconnected, your priorities are seriously out of whack! It happens often in guy/girl relationships, and it needs to be fixed.

It's time to put first things first. Make your family relationships right. Keep them strong. Love your family first and foremost. Every other friendship or relationship comes after God and family.

If you will stay close to your family, your other friendships will have much better balance and strength. You won't be so vulnerable to peer pressure, emotional dependency, or physical temptation. And someday, when you have a family of your own, you will have already learned how to make them your first priority next to God.

Choose family first!

SIXTEEN 16

Choose True Love

So far in this book we've seen God's big picture—preparing us for a wonderful someday. We've also seen many big choices you should make. Think of them:

>Choose "The Right Person at the Right Time"
>Choose God's Will
>Choose Controlled Emotions
>Choose Purity
>Choose "No Touch"
>Choose Family First
>and now...
>*Choose True Love*

Much of what we've covered boils down to understanding the difference between true love and what the Bible calls *lust*. Lust is a sinful, selfish desire for something that is forbidden. Often, in God's Word, lust refers to sexual or physical sin in the relationship between a man and a woman.

Your goal as a Christian should be to allow God's Holy Spirit to control your life rather than allowing your lusts to control you. God says, "This I say then, Walk in the Spirit, and ye shall not fulfil the lust of the flesh" (Galatians 5:16). "But the fruit of the Spirit is love, joy, peace, longsuffering, gentleness, goodness, faith" (Galatians 5:22). A lust-led life is very different than a Spirit-led life.

Even so, a lust-led guy/girl relationship is very dangerous and in many ways opposite of a Spirit-led relationship. We have written this book assuming you long for God's best—hoping and praying that you will allow the Spirit to put down your lust and lead your life in godly directions.

When you understand the difference between lust and true love, it becomes easier to choose true love. It becomes easier to have patience and to wait on God's best. And as we've seen, the world has warped its definition of love for so long that many young Christians do not know the difference. Let's compare the two.

The Difference between Lust and Love

1. **Lust is physical while love is spiritual.** Lust is fed by touching, but love is fed by selflessness. Love is better—it majors on the spiritual side of a relationship.

Sixteen—Choose True Love

2. Lust is temporal while love is eternal. Amnon in 2 Samuel 13 said he "loved" his half-sister, Tamar. Notice in verses 14 and 15: "Howbeit he would not hearken unto her voice: but, being stronger than she, forced her, and lay with her. Then Amnon hated her exceedingly; so that the hatred wherewith he hated her was greater than the love wherewith he had loved her. And Amnon said unto her, Arise, be gone."

Amnon said he loved Tamar, but he did not. It was lust which soon became hatred. Likewise, Samson's immoral relationships were temporal—lust not love. Love is better—it lasts forever.

3. Lust is selfish while love cares for others. Lust is pure selfishness. It's a man's effort to please himself. Lust cares not how the other person feels. Lust only wants to fulfill its natural desires. Love is better—it cares for others.

4. Lust brings guilt while love protects a clear conscience. After lust there is always shame and remorse because of the sin. Love is better—it brings no guilt.

5. Lust says "hurry up" while love says "wait on God." Lust happens quickly, but real love takes time to grow. When Jacob worked for fourteen years to marry his uncle's daughter, Rachel, the Scripture says in Genesis 29:20, "…and they seemed unto him but a few days, for the love he had to her." Lust must be satisfied now. Love is better—it helps you wait.

6. Lust sees no fault; love forgives fault. Lust causes you to think another person is perfect—setting you up for disappointment. Love is not blind; lust is. Love does see weaknesses, but it continues to love. Love is better—it loves you the way you are.

7. Lust thrives on fantasy; love is based upon truth. Lust idolizes and worships another based upon an image that isn't real. Love is better—it is real.

8. Lust fades over time, and love grows over time. Lust is like a shooting star which is bright for a while and then fades away. Have you ever felt like "the better I get to know a certain person, the less I like them"? That is not love. Love intensifies with time. Infatuation and lust wear off. Love is better—it grows.

9. Lust always destroys, but love builds. Lust gradually dismantles your life—like taking a building apart one brick and one board at a time. But love always builds your life and makes you a better person in God's grace. Love is better—it builds.

Be careful! When you experience attraction towards another person—and you will—you must immediately make a choice—lust or love? Lust will take you down a selfish, temporary path of danger. Love will cause you to always do what is spiritually best for you and the other person. Sometimes that will mean the attraction is even resisted or starved and allowed to die.

We're not saying you should try to "fall in love" too soon. But simply that godly love is much different from lust. And yes, even as a young person, while you're just friends, you should love your friends with a Christ-like

Sixteen—Choose True Love

love that helps them be holy, godly, and pure. If you truly love that other person, you will allow the Holy Spirit to crush lust, and you will keep the relationship pure and right in God's eyes.

Practice falling in love—not by allowing infatuation to consume you but by loving God so much that you love others the way He does. Someday, your marital love will grow out of that heart, and true love is like a cute little green tomato—it is a lot richer and more tasteful when allowed to ripen in God's time.

Flee youthful lusts—and choose true love!

SEVENTEEN

Choose "Just Friends"

Honestly, *twitterpation* isn't all that it's cracked up to be. The *girlfriend/boyfriend* thing leaves a lot to be desired. It's a real trap that brings with it danger and disappointment during youth. Hopefully, after reading these chapters, you're figuring this out. It robs you of the blessing of sincere and open-hearted friendship. It makes you feel weird, uncomfortable, awkward, and insecure. It requires you to impress, to fit in, to conform, and to "belong" to someone. It takes you away from other good friends and corners you into exclusivity and obligation. It stirs up emotions that are confusing, frustrating, and difficult to understand. And it risks serious mistakes like impurity and emotional dependency. This is enough to make any sane adult want to run for cover!

Think about all the risks we've talked about—all the dangers that come to youthful relationships that go too far, too fast, too soon. They feel good for a while, but they end up on that double dead end road. It's nice being liked, but over time, these emotional roller coaster rides start to take their toll.

Some young adults spend all of their school and college years going from one relationship to the next—giving their heart to one person after another. Usually these relationships are emotional, physical, lustful, and self-centered. Very few of them actually stay in balance as healthy friendships.

Early in this book we saw God's big picture—that He has a wonderful someday—the right person at the right time. We also saw the big choices that you must make to survive this world of emotions and attractions. We said:

>   Choose "The Right Person at the Right Time"
>   Choose God's Will
>   Choose Controlled Emotions
>   Choose Purity
>   Choose "No Touch"
>   Choose Family First
>   Choose True Love
>   and now...
>   *Choose "Just Friends"*

Wouldn't you like to look back on these years and have no regrets? Doesn't the path of true friendship

Seventeen—Choose "Just Friends"

sound much more appealing than the miserable world of dating and breakups? Regardless of what your culture and peers are doing, you can navigate your young adult years better than most!

At this point, we want to challenge you to make a serious choice:

Choose the "just friends" approach to guy/girl relationships while you are young.

All things considered, this is the safest, wisest, most biblical, most helpful, most Christ-honoring, and most healthy way to approach your youthful attractions. Decide that you won't board the emotional roller coaster. Reject Hollywood's model of "finding the right person." Embrace God's model of "becoming the right person." Rather than obsessing over guys or girls—obsess over God and growing into His image. Obsess over knowing Him and spending time with others who want to know Him. Obsess over becoming who God desires you to become.

During the process, you may find a friend—a guy or girl whom you find interesting and even attractive. This isn't wrong unless you allow it to become wrong. Decide together to make it a helpful friendship. Decide to keep God and family first. Decide to stay emotionally balanced and physically pure and apart. Decide to keep

> Rather than obsessing over guys or girls— obsess over God and growing into His image.

your friendship Christ-honoring and wholesome. Help each other, encourage each other, uplift each other spiritually. Sharpen, strengthen, and support each other. Rejoice with each other, pray for each other, and enjoy the wonderful benefits of biblical friendship while you avoid all the painful traps of carnal relationships.

And all the while, look forward! Anticipate. Envision. Pray. Prepare. Grow. Surrender. Keep your eyes on the prize—God's perfect will—the right person at the right time! Stay focused on becoming the best person you can become. Focus on helping your friends to do the same.

This is the very BEST way to become the right person!

When you choose "just friends" you win! You gain more than you realize. Think of these qualities of true friendships—the things you should be for your friends, and the things you gain by having godly friends:

1. A friend is kind (Proverbs 18:24). Friends treat each other considerately. Jesus was kind. Friendly people speak to people and smile. Jesus reached out in friendship to Zachaeus, the woman at the well, Peter, and many others.

2. A friend is faithful. His love never fails. He loves you through thick and thin, when you are up or down, when you are close to God and when you are backslidden. Distance and time will not separate real friends.

I (Mike) heard a story of a football player who played wide receiver in a championship football game.

Seventeen—Choose "Just Friends"

He had a chance to catch a winning touchdown pass in the last seconds of the game but dropped the ball. His own team got off the bench and left him when he sat down after the game. But one friend quietly walked over and just sat by him. A real friend is one who still loves you even after you blow it. It is not a conditional love. A friend loves you no matter what. He will never forsake you (Proverbs 27:10A).

Don't misunderstand. You should still separate from bad influences. Psalm 1 and Proverbs 1 are very clear that we must distance ourselves from fools, scorners, and ungodly people.

3. A friend makes you a better person (Proverbs 27:17). A friend always lifts you up and pulls you to higher ground. A friend always urges you to do right. A friend would never influence you to do something against your conscience.

4. A friend is knit to your heart (1 Samuel 18:1). This friendship is a gift from God and encourages your heart in godly things.

5. A friend can share friends. Jesus said "our friend Lazarus is sick." Jesus shared His friends. A true friend doesn't have problems with friends having other friends. There is no jealousy or possessiveness. Immaturity says, "We're best friends." It's grade school mentality to insist on being someone's "best friend."

6. A friend expresses love. Secret love has no place in real friendships (Proverbs 27:5). Tell friends why they are important to you, and express your gratitude. This isn't about saying "I love you." It's about living it.

7. A friend is willing to wound. "Faithful are the wounds of a friend…" (Proverbs 27:6). It is the responsibility of a friend to correct or even kindly rebuke when tough love needs to be spoken. You may feel awkward confronting a friend about a bad spirit, lies, or hidden sin. But true love will say the right thing to strengthen another.

8. A friend strengthens others in God. Jonathan strengthened the hand of his friend David "in God" (1 Samuel 23:16). He directed David's attention off his problems and onto God's power. Three thousand enemy soldiers could not locate David, but one good friend did. This is one reason why you need to be a strong Christian, so you have strength to give in times of need.

9. A friend is willing to be second. A true friend helps another succeed and is willing to be out of the spotlight. Read about Jonathan's friendship to David—he was the model friend in the Bible. David was closer to God because of Jonathan. Jonathan was even willing to give up his right to the throne for David. What an example of biblical friendship.

10. A friend rejoices in blessings. Whether it's a good grade, a position on a team, or a special honor—a true friend will always be able to rejoice when God does something good for another.

11. A friend praises his friends. Proverbs 27:2 says, "Let another man praise thee…." Friends look for the good and compliment others. They avoid gossip and tearing people down. They don't have to be sarcastic or rude toward others to make themselves look better. They rejoice when another is encouraged or uplifted.

12. A friend doesn't overstay his welcome. It is possible to be around someone too much. Proverbs 27:7 says, "The full soul loatheth the honeycomb…." Too much of a good friendship is unhealthy for both people. Let your heart hunger for more—that's a good thing.

13. A friend gives biblical counsel (Proverbs 27:9). To be a good friend, you must know God's Word and be able to give biblical wisdom. You will influence your friends by your words and presence.

14. A friend is sensitive. Proverbs 27:14 says, "He that blesseth his friend with a loud voice, rising early in the morning, it shall be counted a curse to him." A friend tries to be sensitive and responsive to the spirit and heart of another.

15. A friend sharpens. Proverbs 27:17 says, "Iron sharpeneth iron; so a man sharpeneth the countenance of his friend." The greatest words I (Mike) ever had written in my college yearbook were by a roommate who said, "Our college has become a better place because you came." Are your friends better Christians because of you?

16. A friend helps through trials. "A friend loveth at all times, and a brother is born for adversity" (Proverbs 17:17). Good friends are there with biblical support and prayer when someone goes through a tough time.

One poet wrote:
"I went out to find a friend,
But could not find one there,
I went out to be a friend
And friends were everywhere."

It has been said, "Happy is the man who has a friend. Happier is the man who is a friend. Happiest is the man who has a friend and is a friend."

"A man that hath friends must shew himself friendly: and there is a friend that sticketh closer than a brother" (Proverbs 18:24). Since friendship starts with friendliness, here are ten practical ways to show yourself friendly:

1. Treat everyone politely.
2. Learn to smile.
3. Invite people to sit with you.
4. Share with others.
5. Introduce new people to others.
6. Reach out to new people.
7. Look for ways to serve others.
8. Think of ways to encourage others.
9. Write lots of thank you notes.
10. Think of encouraging things to say.

The best foundation you can build is to be a friend to others. Be a real friend to those in your youth group

Seventeen—Choose "Just Friends"

or school. As God sees you being who you should be, in His time He will most likely knit your soul close to a member of the opposite gender. At that time, it won't take much to build a strong and healthy relationship with the right person—you will have already laid a strong foundation by being his or her *friend*.

In many broken homes, the husband and wife were never "just friends" first. They entered into a relationship of lust, failed to restrain emotion, gave in to physical desires, and found themselves greatly lacking the right friendship to sustain their marriage. Don't let this happen to you. Friendship is the glue that holds all relationships together—so master the art while you are still young.

Friendship is sweet, but many so-called "dating relationships" are bitter. Until your frontal lobe is done and your younger years are behind you, why not choose to stay "just friends."

# Think About It
Chapters 15–17

Assignment for Personal Application

Find a quiet place, a blank paper, and think through these practical exercises. Consider sharing this exercise with a parent, friend, a group of friends, or a teacher.

1. Think through last week and write out how much time you spent with your parents. Was it enough or too little? What can you do about it?

2. Describe why you think the devil fights your relationships at home.

3. Describe in your own words the difference between lust and love.

4. Make a list of all the reasons why the "just friends" approach is the best approach to young adult relationships when marriage is not an option.

5. Of the sixteen qualities of friendship, list the people you know that would fit most or all of the qualities on the list. Commit to developing friendships with those people.

Memorize these verses: "Honour thy father and mother; which is the first commandment with promise; That it may be well with thee, and thou mayest live long on the earth" (Ephesians 6:2–3).

PART THREE

Get the Details Right

*The remaining chapters of this book
contain stand-alone topics of advice
and helpful information as you strive to
develop godly friendships.*

EIGHTEEN

Becoming the Right Person

One of the engaged couples in my (Mike) church recently looked for an apartment for after their wedding. They soon discovered that all the furnished apartments were more expensive than the unfurnished. The furnished were more appealing to the couple because these apartments were fully prepared and ready to be used.

This is what God means when He says, "That the man of God may be perfect, throughly furnished unto all good works" (2 Timothy 3:17). God wants you to be ready to go—fully prepared for your future calling and family when they arrive.

"Prepare thy work without, and make it fit for thyself in the field; and afterwards build thine house" (Proverbs 24:27). "The preparations of the heart in man, and the answer of the tongue, is from the LORD" (Proverbs 16:1). Much of this book has been about helping you prepare—to become ready as you enter young adult life and become eligible for a serious relationship that could lead to marriage. God desires for you to be "furnished" and ready for Him to use.

The Bible speaks much about "preparing." The disciples spent three years with Jesus preparing. Jesus spent thirty years preparing for the ministry. Moses spent forty years in the desert preparing to lead God's people. Paul spent three years in the Arabian desert preparing for his life's work.

> God desires for you to be "furnished" and ready for Him to use.

The more prepared you are for future roles, the more confidence you will have when you begin those roles. There are many things you can do now to prepare for the future. Here are a few thoughts:

How Girls Can Prepare

1. Learn to be a virtuous woman. Proverbs 31 talks about all the ways a virtuous woman takes care of and serves those she loves. She is very creative and industrious.

2. Learn to keep a nice home. This will be a blessing to your parents and to your future family and ministry. Keep your room and your closet the way you would like your future home to be kept. Learn to create a nice atmosphere.

3. Learn to prepare nice meals. Everybody likes to sit down and enjoy a meal with people they love. In your future home, your meals will be a blessing to your whole family. The Bible tells us to be "given to hospitality"—and there's no better time to learn this art than now.

4. Learn to be thrifty with money. Financial problems are one of the biggest reasons for marital strife. Everyone has to live by a budget, and learning to be money conscious now will give you a big head start. Practice learning the shopping needs and budget practices for running a household.

5. Learn to work with children. Whether through babysitting, serving in a nursery or Sunday school, learn how to teach, discipline, and nurture children. Learn from good mothers and older ladies in your church.

6. Learn to read good books. There are many good books on the Christian life, finding God's will, and parenting. Read the biographies of great Christians or books on godly womanhood. Give much more time to reading than to idle things like online social networking, texting, or games. God teaches us to get wisdom, understanding, and knowledge—they all work together!

7. Learn to be organized. Organize your room, your closet, your locker, and your whole life. God delights in order. Learning self-discipline in these areas will make you a better person in all aspects of your life.

How Guys Can Prepare

1. **Learn to be a godly man.** Through the Bible and many other good books you can learn what manhood is about. Learn about masculinity, play sports, build endurance, courage, and strength. Have a masculine hairstyle, and dress in manly clothing. Learn to walk, sit, stand, talk, and shake hands like a man. Be distinctly masculine for God's glory.

2. **Learn how to handle finances.** Learn how to open and use a checking and savings account. Learn about loans, family budgets, and how to save money. You will one day be responsible for providing and caring for your family. The more you learn now, the more prepared you will be. Ask your dad how he handles your family's finances. Get him to teach you how to pay bills and how to make it all work.

3. **Learn how to protect others.** One day, you will need to be able to protect your family both physically and spiritually. You should learn how to make people feel secure and cared for. A young man should know how to keep his family safe at night and in public places.

4. **Learn to work with children.** Learn how to teach, discipline, nurture, and play with children. Watch good fathers, and see how they interact with their families.

5. **Learn to be a leader.** You are preparing to lead your family and others. Learn to set an example. Learn

Eighteen—Becoming the Right Person

to exert a positive peer pressure rather than giving in to negative. Learn to take a stand no matter what it costs.

6. Learn to read good books. There are many good books on the Christian life, finding God's will, Christian manhood, and spiritual leadership. Read the biographies of great Christians. Give much more time to reading than to idle things like video games. God teaches us to get wisdom, understanding, and knowledge—they all work together!

7. Learn to be organized. Organize your room, your closet, your locker, and your whole life. God delights in order. Learning self-discipline in these areas will make you a better person in all of your life.

20 Qualities Everyone Should Pursue

1. Learn to be spiritual. Seek first God's kingdom (Matthew 6:33). Desire to do God's will more than anything. Be involved in winning others, serving God, and walking faithfully.

2. Learn to develop godly character. This is subconsciously doing right, or, as someone put it, "right by reflex." This includes the ability to say no to sin, get up on time, be on time, etc. Character is who you are when no one is around.

3. Learn to be loyal. Start with God and authorities. Learn to take a stand and to speak in defense of those who love you. Don't put up with gossip and bad attitudes.

4. Learn to treat your family well. If you treat your parents and siblings right, you will one day treat your spouse and children right.

5. Learn stability. Learn how to be content and to wait on God. Don't be constantly reconsidering good decisions, looking for the next fun thing, or changing your mind about what you believe. Learn to establish your heart in God—don't have a "plan B." Be constant and consistent—in your attitude, your service, your respect, and your treatment of others. Learn to not quit when things get tough!

6. Learn to develop convictions. Do you know what you believe and why? It's time to establish your own convictions and personal standards. Learn to stand on what is right and not to waver. Have convictions as strong as those of the guy or girl to whom you may be attracted!

7. Learn to look sharp. Have a clean and appropriate appearance. Learn to dress right for various occasions. Guys—keep a short haircut, dress sharp, and avoid worldly styles. Cut your nails, wash your hands, polish your shoes, iron your shirts. Girls—be modest, feminine, and godly in your appearance.

8. Learn to set and pursue goals. Set your direction in life. Decide what you would like to learn, read, do, and experience to become the right person. Set goals for sharing the Gospel with people, serving God faithfully, giving, and helping others—and then pursue those goals until they are fulfilled. Then set new goals!

Eighteen—Becoming the Right Person

Proverbs 29:18, "Where there is no vision, the people perish…." Today's average high school senior upon graduation has no idea what to be or do. This is a sad testimony of their walk with God.

9. Learn to be unselfish and submissive. Begin to live for others. Give other people their way, just because you want to be nice. Think of others before yourself. This is what it takes to have a strong family someday.

10. Learn to be respectful and attentive. Build great listening skills in church, in school, or when another person is speaking.

11. Learn to make good decisions biblically. Consider how you make decisions. Are they based upon emotion, impulse, and personal desires? Or are they based upon God's Word, the leading of the Spirit, and the wise thing to do? Learn to do the right thing no matter how hard it is or what it costs.

12. Learn to control your temper. People who cannot control themselves do hurtful things to others. God wants us to be angry at sin but loving towards people.

13. Learn to have a great testimony. Past friendships, past trouble, present friends, dress, music, lifestyle, posture, countenance, habits, and outward appearances all impact what others think of you. This is called your *name* or your *testimony,* and you must learn to protect it. God says, "A good name is rather to be chosen than great riches, and loving favour rather than silver and gold" (Proverbs 22:1).

14. Learn to work hard. Life is hard work, especially family life. Take value in the work you do. If you wait until the last minute, sloppily do your work, and then don't care about the outcome, you're developing lazy character. Learn how to pour your best into everything you're given to do. Develop a solid work ethic, and don't be afraid of hard work.

15. Learn to take care of your body. Stay healthy, eat right, discipline yourself. Your body belongs to God and is the temple of the Holy Spirit. Bad health habits will greatly limit your usefulness to God.

16. Learn to tithe and to trust God. If a man will rob from God, that man should not be trusted. Of everything that God gives to you, give Him back at least ten percent through your local church.

17. Learn to be real and sincere. Stop playing games, and refuse to be a hypocrite. Too many young adults act one way around friends and another way around authorities. This will only make your future worse!

18. Learn to be understanding and accepting of others. Not everybody is just like you or your close friends. That doesn't make you better. Godly people love and treat everybody with decency and respect.

19. Learn to get along with others. Some people seem to relish conflict. Like that Charlie Brown character, Pig Pen, everywhere they go they have a little dust cloud of fights, gossip, and strife following them. When there is no strife, they make it up—it's like Dracula needing

Eighteen—Becoming the Right Person

blood! They must have it. Don't be this way and don't spend time with these people.

20. Learn to have discernment and discretion. Discernment is the ability to perceive and see things through God's wisdom. Discretion is knowing what to say, how to say it, and when to say it. This is the opposite of being obnoxious, foolish, flirtatious, and boisterous. It's not having to be the center of attention, but letting God be the center of attention. For a young lady, the Bible calls this a "meek and quiet spirit" (1 Peter 3:4).

Notice good looks and wealth are not on the list. External good looks should be a byproduct of internal qualities! Place your focus on being right *inside*, and God will give you a great countenance!

Young Abraham Lincoln was reading a book one day and someone said, "Hello, Abe. Are you studying law? Do you expect to be President some day?" Abe replied, "I don't know, but I am going to be ready for anything God would have for me to do!"

Are you spending your youth on folly and pointless things, or are you preparing? There's nothing wrong with an occasional video game or wholesome relaxing activity, but make sure a major part of your life is given to preparing and becoming the right person.

Remember, youth is about *becoming* the right person! If you will become this kind of person, you will be attracted to this type of person, and they will be attracted to you.

NINETEEN
Setting the Right Pace

If you choose the "just friends" approach to guy/girl relationships until you are ready for a more serious relationship, then you must understand the principle of *pace*. Healthy relationships set a careful pace, but unhealthy ones progress forward too quickly and self destruct.

Setting a right pace will help you avoid emotional dependency, physical temptation, over-familiarity, and relational confusion. You must think of it this way—you are running a *marathon*, not a *sprint*! The right pace will help you arrive at that wonderful someday in one piece—prepared and ready for your future spouse and God's calling.

Many good relationships have been ruined because of too much time spent together. Yes, you can spend too much time with someone you really like. Familiarity breeds contempt. If you are *always* with your friend, soon arguments arise about the silliest things, and the relationship becomes emotional and self-centered. Obsessing over a good friendship is like obsessing over cotton candy! A little cotton candy is great, but have it for three meals a day for a week and you'll be in pretty bad shape.

A good relationship is like a bee. A bee flies all day gathering nectar from flowers, then brings his supply into the hive to make honey. A wise young adult will spend a lot of time away from a friend, gathering news and experiences so that when they are together they have something fresh and new about which to talk.

Do you remember how exciting it was when you saw a friend or relative after not seeing them in years? The talk was fast, full of news, updates, and excitement. Time spent together with friends ought to be the same. There should be enough "apart time" to keep the relationship balanced and interesting.

The question we are most often asked about guy/girl relationships is this: "How do we set the right pace?"

First we'll share a couple of big concepts, and then a few practical tips.

Make Open Commitments about Pace

You and your friend need to have a focused talk, and your parents should be a part of it if they desire. There's

Nineteen—Setting the Right Pace

nothing wrong with admitting that you are interested in each other. Why not agree to just be good friends? Make a commitment to each other that you will keep your relationship Christ-centered, family first, no touch, emotionally balanced, and physically pure. Agree to talk about spiritual things, to encourage each other in the Lord, and to spend enough time apart. Agree to not develop a sense of obligation to each other.

Many guy/girl friendships turn into obligations. You *must* sit together, walk together, talk together, etc. It's an unspoken contract. So, talk about it, and agree to not let this happen.

Talk about how much time you will spend together, and set limits. Decide how much you will talk on the phone, text message, or connect over a social networking site. Decide how often you will write or email each other. Set intentional limits upon yourselves. This is a wise and mature approach. When it is mutual, you will help each other keep your commitment, and your authorities will marvel at your maturity and depth of responsibility.

So, step one in setting the right pace is to sit down, talk together, and place restrictions upon yourselves. Let's talk about step two.

Ask for Help from Parents and Authorities

No matter how hard you try, you will sometimes fail at step one. This is where step two comes in. You must have outside help! Relationships can very quickly get out of balance. Emotions can change, feelings can grow stronger, and before you know it, you're putting someone before God, before family, and before other important priorities in life.

This is vital: *other people will see your misplaced priorities before you do!* Your parents will notice a change in your spirit, your friendship, and your behavior. You will start to show those seventeen signs of emotional dependency that we studied in chapter ten. But you will be blind to it at first. In fact, you'll even get irritated and upset when your parents or others point it out.

> Other people will see your misplaced priorities before you do!

Guaranteed, every time, when you get defensive and irritated at this, they are right! You are going too far, too fast, too soon in this relationship. When we get irritated at someone for telling us something we don't want to hear, it's usually because they are right!

In these cases, the only way to really set the pace is to *let someone else set it for you.*

When I (Cary) started having an interest in my wife, Dana, we were seniors in high school. We really liked each other! The problem was, it was a little early to get too serious. We still had college and much to learn before we could be married and start our lives together. Pace was a big issue for us! In fact, without it, our relationship would have self-destructed. We would have moved too

Nineteen—Setting the Right Pace

fast, too soon—and we probably wouldn't have ended up together in God's will.

How did we make it happen? We took the two steps we're sharing. First we talked about it and made some tough choices. We agreed not to touch. We agreed to keep God first. We promised to have other friends and to keep our relationship "group friendly." We made all of the choices we've discussed in this book.

But even then, we sometimes got out of balance! Even with our good intentions, we found ourselves desiring to talk more, spend more time together, eat dinner at each other's houses more often. Given our way, we would have overdone it! We would have spent more time together than was healthy.

What made the difference? Our parents. They slowed us down whenever we started going too fast.

Have you ever seen a student-driving vehicle? In these vehicles, the *student* has a brake and a steering wheel on the driver's side, but the *instructor* has a brake and a steering wheel on the passenger's side! Why? So the instructor can intervene when the student doesn't do the right thing.

So there you are, in the student vehicle of guy/girl relationships. Who is your *instructor*? More importantly, have you given your instructor a brake and a wheel on their side of the vehicle? When you start down the road of this relationship, you will most likely to go too fast—everyone does. You will make mistakes—everyone does.

You will try to make some wrong turns, and if someone doesn't help you, you're going to crash!

Do you want to crash? Or do you want help?

Your parents and spiritual leaders should have one hand on their wheel and one foot on their brake throughout all of your youthful relationships. They should be able to slow you down, pull you over, and even turn you around if they need to.

In our lives, our parents often said, "No, she cannot come over." "No, you cannot call her." "No, he cannot come with us." And to be honest—we HATED it! We didn't understand. We thought they were unreasonable. And we generally suffered through those times. But look at the result. We didn't crash!

Nineteen years later, we're still moving forward, madly in love, and best friends. That's the product of having the *right pace*.

Two steps to a right pace—*set boundaries for yourself*, and *get outside help*. You must have them both, and you must submit to authority when you think they are being unreasonable. They are acting in your best interest. And they are right!

Considering the Right Boundaries

We strongly urge you to ask your parents for guidelines and restrictions when it comes to these matters. They

Nineteen—SETTING THE RIGHT PACE

know you, and they will be sensitive to your needs. Do exactly what they say in the specifics, but, here are some general and practical suggestions for setting a reasonable pace. You might talk to them about these things:

1. **Limit face-to-face time.** Decide when to be together and when to be apart. Don't *always* be together. Balance your time.

2. **Limit verbal communication.** Set boundaries for how *many* phone calls and how *long* they should be. Frequent, long, drawn out phone calls are bad for young hearts and generally serve no real purpose!

3. **Limit non-verbal communication.** Set limits on notes, emails, text messages, and social networking. Don't allow late night communication or non-stop messaging. And what little messaging you do should be completely open and honoring to the Lord.

4. **Sit with family in church.** You'll get more out of the message; your family will appreciate it; and you'll stay more in balance in your friendships. It's very hard to hear a Bible message when your twitterpated heart is going haywire for the person next to you.

5. **Stay "group friendly."** There's something really cool about two young people who like each other but aren't consumed with each other. And this reveals it! Have fun with the whole group—whether friends or family. Don't be alone and disconnected from family and friends.

6. Keep communication accountable. You're going to love this one! Don't write a note, a text, an email, or anything else that someone in authority couldn't read and be pleased with.

This past Christmas my (Cary) son planned to give a young lady a Christmas gift, and she had one for him as well. When the gift exchange was about to take place, unbeknownst to my son, both sets of parents assembled to enjoy the moment. We caught them off guard a little, but what a delight it was to see them laugh and proceed in giving each other their gifts.

Matters became even funnier when both dads grabbed the Christmas cards and began to read them. Our senior highers lightly laughed again, and said nothing of it. It was both cute and cool at the same time! How great that two young people could have that kind of open friendship in front of their parents. I believe that pleases the Lord.

One of my favorite things to do in our youth group is to walk into a public meeting with a folded piece of paper, hold it up with a very stern look on my face, and say, "I found a note!"

Instantly about half of the teens in the room freeze in fear. Their blood pressure rises, their hearts pound, and they panic! These teens start immediately wondering, "Is it mine? How much trouble am I in? What exactly did I write?" It's a terrifying experience for them.

I know—I'm sick. But it's hilarious! The other half of the room—the ones with clear consciences—have

Nineteen—Setting the Right Pace

nothing to fear. They sit there thinking, "Well, if it's one of mine, no big deal, I don't have anything to hide."

Which group would you be in? What if we could reach out of this book and pick up your cell phone, your computer, or read the communications you've been exchanging? Would you be embarrassed? Would the Lord be honored?

If you keep your communications accountable and pure, there should be nothing to fear!

Pace Is Important

Here's a simple illustration of going too fast:

> *Day 1: Bill likes Sally and asks to sit by her at church.*
>
> *Day 2: Bill calls Sally on phone and says he likes her.*
>
> *Day 3: Bill goes over to Sally's and gives her his ring. They are now going steady.*
>
> *Day 4: Bill tells Sally he loves her.*
>
> *Day 5: Bill talks to Sally about their future together and maybe engagement.*
>
> *Day 6: Bill and Sally break up and never want to see each other again.*
>
> *Day 7: Sally has a party on her twelfth birthday, but she's too depressed to enjoy it!*

This may be over-simplified and humorous, but it's also pretty close to reality. How many times have you seen it this way? They went too fast, too soon, and messed up a good friendship that God could have blessed.

Making the "just friends" approach work will require you to set the right pace. And when you can't set it, you must get help. Remember, you're running a marathon, not a sprint. Let a healthy pace be your goal and let those who love you help you make it happen.

TWENTY

Advantages of "Just Friends"

In some young minds, having a boyfriend or girlfriend is an *absolute essential*—right up there with water, oxygen, food, and sleep. As soon as one relationship ends, a replacement *must be found*. Some people just can't deal with the thought of going even a few days without a "special someone." It's a kind of emotional bondage—a self-imposed prison in which they lock themselves. These "boyfriends and girlfriends" are not real friends, they're more like security blankets. It's not so much about liking someone but rather about *being liked*. In other words, *not* having a boyfriend or girlfriend is just *not* an option—it's an unbearable thought for some!

Not only is that a needless way to live, this is just a burdensome way to traverse your youth. It brings a lot of unnecessary worry and self-imposed pressure. There is a better way!

If you take our advice and go with the "just friends" approach to guy/girl relationships, there are many advantages. You spare yourself much heartache, heartbreak, and emotional trauma. In addition to this, you avoid all the potential pitfalls that we've already talked about.

Honestly, there are some great advantages to "just friends"—to not being in an exclusive boyfriend/girlfriend relationship until the right time. We thought we would highlight a few advantages in this chapter. This is a glimpse of the good side of not being "tied down":

1. You have more time for spiritual things. The average young adult leads such a busy life that they have to *make time* for devotions. How great it would be to dig into the Bible and find the answers to your questions! Time and energy you would invest into an obligated relationship, you can now invest into walking with God and knowing Him.

2. You can see other couples' mistakes more clearly. People who are overdosed on twitterpation never realize just how ridiculous they look—until they see it in another couple. Watch the mistakes of others and make mental notes to avoid them.

3. You can spend time with others without pressure. When you do not have a boyfriend or girlfriend you are "free" to talk to other friends. Many guys and girls have been made miserable by being "tied down." They are obligated to one person and miss many other

Twenty—Advantages of "Just Friends"

wonderful friendships as well as opportunities to learn valuable lessons.

   4. You have more money to fill people's needs with. When guys and girls are not spending money on each other, they can invest that same money into God's work or other important priorities—like saving for a car or for college.

   5. You have less gossip spread about you. Maybe it is jealousy or envy, but usually when a couple becomes interested in each other, there is a greater chance that people will talk about them—and not always truthfully.

   6. You do not have to go through the heartbreak of "breaking up." Oh, the tears we have seen! Breaking off relationships causes more tears than anything else. A person without a boyfriend or girlfriend can spare themselves the agony.

   7. You can focus on more important relationships. The time and energy you would invest into a guy or girl can be invested into your family, leading others to Christ, discipling new Christians, and serving the Lord.

   8. You grow more because your heart is focused on Christ. You hear more in church, learn more in classes, and generally absorb more wisdom because your heart and mind are free of infatuation and distraction.

   9. You avoid a ton of temptation. You don't have the same degree of temptation regarding losing your purity or becoming too emotionally involved.

10. You enjoy your life more because you have fewer relational burdens. You can attend activities, events, and church without being strapped to one person and feeling obligated to be together. You don't have to work through misunderstandings, problems, and issues. You are free to just enjoy life!

Face it, there will be many periods during your youth when you are not interested in anyone. Can you be okay with that? We hope so! No need to force it.

Don't be impatient with God. Perhaps during these times of waiting He is preparing a man or woman to be just what you need. Perhaps He is preparing you to be what someone else needs. Maybe a guy or girl would be the single distraction that keeps you from growing in God's grace at this point in your life.

If you are interested in someone, think through these advantages. You might decide to keep it light—keep it "just friends"—if only to spare yourself the burdens and to benefit from these good things. If you do not have a guy/girl friendship right now, count your blessings, and enjoy it! Your time will come.

Twenty—Advantages of "Just Friends"

Think About It
Chapters 18–20

Assignment for Personal Application

Find a quiet place, a blank paper, and think through these practical exercises. Consider sharing this exercise with a parent, friend, a group of friends, or a teacher.

1. List the character qualities you most need to work on developing in your life. Next to each one, write out one thing you will do to help make a step in the right direction.

2. Do you need to talk with a friend about pace? If so, make the commitment to do it, and write out the list of things you will suggest doing to set the right pace.

3. Describe in your life who must help you set the right pace—what people? Before you talk to your friend about the list in question 2, talk to these people and get their input.

4. In your own words, describe why pace is important.

5. Of the ten advantages of not having a guy/girl relationship, which ones are you enjoying right now? List them.

Memorize these verses: "See then that ye walk circumspectly, not as fools, but as wise, Redeeming the time, because the days are evil. Wherefore be ye not unwise, but understanding what the will of the Lord is" (Ephesians 5:15–17).

TWENTY-ONE

Treating People Right

Whether therefore ye eat, or drink, or whatsoever ye do, do all to the glory of God.—1 CORINTHIANS 10:31

This chapter is primarily about etiquette—knowing how to act in various situations. It's about godly and respectful behavior, not only in your guy/girl relationships, but in many aspects of life. As you become the right person, it's important to learn the basics of decency, respectfulness, and the appropriate treatment of others.

Kids can be mean to each other. Kids can be thoughtless and self-centered at times. But you're not a kid anymore. You're transitioning into adulthood, and these rules of etiquette are a big part of that transition.

Every young person longs to be thought of as mature. Wouldn't you love for people to genuinely respect you and think highly of you when your name is mentioned? Then pay careful attention to this list. A young adult who practices these things really gets noticed, because so few live this way.

This list has major implications for your life—not only in respect to guy/girl relationships, but in getting a job, getting promoted, and in a thousand other good things. Well-mannered people are hard to find. If you are one, you will be most blessed! As God instructs us to "put on" Christ and "put off" the old man, these lists are not meant to be legalistic, but rather just to suggest some practical and appropriate ways to think of others.

(This list is an excerpt from Cary's book *Different by Design*—a personal study of biblical living. It is available at www.strivingtogether.com)

Basic Rules of Etiquette
Between Guys and Girls
Do

- Keep your conversation and words appropriate and respectful.
- Focus your attention on being polite and respectful.
- Men—Open the door for a lady.
- Men—Offer help when you see it is needed.
- Men—Offer your seat to a lady.
- Men—Always acknowledge and greet a girl's parents.
- Men—Look a girl in the eyes.

Twenty-One—Treating People Right

- Men—Offer your umbrella to a lady if it is raining.
- Men—Offer your suit jacket to a girl if it is cold.
- Men—Open a lady's car door and wait there until she is seated.
- Men—When a lady drops something, help her pick it up.
- Men—Walk on the outside of the sidewalk when with a lady.
- Men—Only shake hands if a lady extends her hand first.
- Men—Ask a girl's father for permission before writing or calling her. (This includes email and text too.)
- Men—Respect your parents' and her parents' wishes in every area.
- Ladies—Maintain a meek and quiet spirit.
- Ladies—Maintain a godly presence in physical posture and dress.
- Ladies—Seek your parents' approval before responding to a guy.

DON'T

- Men—Don't let a lady carry boxes or large items.
- Men—Don't touch a lady, unless to help her recover from a fall.
- Men—Don't walk behind a lady on the stairway.
- Men—Don't spend time with a girl without her dad's permission.

- Ladies—Don't call or text guys.
- Ladies—Don't order the most expensive item on the menu.
- Ladies—Don't try to be the center of attention.
- Ladies—Don't touch guys, even jokingly.
- Ladies—Don't be forward or flirtatious.

Friends and Social Gatherings
Do
- Let people formulate their own opinions of others.
- Speak positively of people who are not present.
- Think before you speak.
- Refrain from bodily noises.
- Thank the host of a function.
- Make eye contact with others when talking.
- Show genuine interest in what others are saying.
- Learn how to ask questions and carry on conversation.
- Invite others "on the sidelines" to be involved socially.
- Politely introduce your friends and family to others.
- Defer the flow of conversation to elders or to those in authority.
- Stand straight, sit up straight, and focus your attention on others.

Twenty-One—Treating People Right

- Graciously accept compliments and defer praise to God and others.
- Men—Give a firm handshake to other men. (No dead fish!)

Don't

- Don't give attention to one person when others are around.
- Don't lose your temper or raise your voice.
- Don't discuss your "breakups" with everyone.
- Don't talk badly about your friends, family, or parents.
- Don't point out other people's bad manners.
- Don't brag about yourself.
- Don't whine and complain.
- Don't joke racially.
- Don't tell jokes that may embarrass people.
- Don't mock people for things they would not laugh at themselves.
- Don't mock people for something they cannot change.
- Don't monopolize or dominate a conversation.
- Don't gossip or conjecture about others.
- Men—Don't joke or talk inappropriately about ladies.
- Men—Don't participate with inappropriate talk or joking.
- Ladies—Don't ask the question, "Does this make me look fat?"

Cell Phones and Phone Calls

Do

- Turn your phone off when in church, restaurants, meetings, etc.
- Immediately give your name and greet the person you are calling.
- Be polite and speak clearly.
- Say "excuse me" when interrupting a conversation to take a call.
- End a call before trying to communicate with someone else.
- Respect other people's time.
- Take responsibility to end a conversation if you started it.

Don't

- Don't talk loudly in public places.
- Don't take calls at the table or in a restaurant.
- Don't take calls while you are talking with someone, if possible.
- Don't say anything inappropriate over the phone or in a text.
- Don't call early, late, or at "dinner time," unless it is an emergency.
- Men—Don't call, text, or email a girl without her dad's permission.
- Ladies—Don't call, text, or email guys.
- Ladies—Don't accept calls from guys without parental permission.

Everyday Speech and Conversation

Do

- Be gracious by using words like "please," "thank you," and "excuse me."
- Respond to authority with "sir" and "ma'am."
- Use your speech to encourage and edify others.

Don't

- Don't be afraid to say "I'm sorry, will you forgive me?"
- Don't respond in sarcasm to a serious question.
- Don't use slang terms or gangster language.
- Don't use euphemisms—words used in place of offensive words (dang, darn it, jeez, frickin', freakin', gosh, golly, heck, etc.).

When with Guests and New Acquaintances

Do

- Stand when a visitor or guest walks into the room.
- Introduce yourself and shake the guest's hand when appropriate.
- Learn and practice polite small talk.
- Introduce someone by telling their name and your relationship with them.

Don't

- Men—Don't take off your tie when you are with company, out of respect.
- Don't ask questions that might make a guest uncomfortable.

Parents and Authority

Do
- Be respectful, obedient, and give honor.
- Maintain eye contact, and listen intently when being spoken to.
- Respect authority with your posture and your facial expressions.
- Prefer and serve authority with a sincere heart.
- Show initiative with chores and acts of kindness.
- Express thankfulness constantly.

Don't
- Don't laugh or mumble under your breath.
- Don't leave the room or walk away when being spoken to.
- Don't withdraw from family relationships.
- Don't heave or sigh.
- Don't roll your eyes.
- Don't participate in dishonoring treatment of authority.

Letters, Notes, and Emails

Do
- Send handwritten thank you notes for any gifts or acts of kindness.
- In a thank you note…
  - Greet the giver (Dear <Name>).
  - Express your gratitude (Thank you for…).

- State how you will use what they have given you.
- Refer to the past and mention the future (It was great to…and I hope to…).
- Thank them again (Thanks again for…).
- Regards (Sincerely)
- Make thank you letters about them, not about you.
- Use blue or black ink in formal writing.
- Write legibly, and use correct grammar and structure.
- Refrain from typing personal notes if possible.

Don't
- Don't use a hard-to-read font or color.
- Don't state the obvious (e.g., "I am just writing to say").
- Don't directly mention money but rather thank them for their generosity or kindness.
- Don't lie about liking a gift, instead compliment the thoughtfulness/generosity of the giver.
- Don't type emails in all caps—this is like yelling.
- Don't gossip in notes and emails.

General/Other

Do
- Make sure your shoes are always clean and polished.

Just Friends

- Stand when someone in authority enters a room.
- Stand to greet someone who approaches your table.
- Use names (people like to hear their own name).
- If you don't know a name, introduce yourself.
- When hearing a new name, try to use it right away.
- Cover your mouth to cough, and excuse yourself if necessary.
- Cover your mouth with a tissue or napkin when sneezing.
- Stand and sit up straight—posture and body language speak loudly.
- Keep your mouth closed when you are not talking.
- Men—Stand when a lady enters the room.
- Men—Shake hands firmly, and make eye contact.

Don't

- Don't pick anything—nose, ears, teeth, fingernails.
- Don't ask dating couples when they're getting married.
- Don't ask married couples when they're planning to have children.
- Don't ask a woman when her baby is due.
- Ladies—Don't wear things that accentuate your body inappropriately.

Dress for Success

Culture is continually wearing sloppier and sleazier clothing, and many young adults have stopped valuing appropriateness and modesty in dress—failing to connect that their appearance impacts their friends and their personal testimony. In other words, *how you dress* has a direct connection with who you are *becoming* and *how other people see you*! If you dress sloppy or sensually, it is a reflection of your heart, your influences, your friends, and your future. If you desire to stay pure, have godly friendships, and set a right example, these things will be obvious in your appearance.

In Matthew 11:7-9, Jesus is speaking about John the Baptist. And while the central context of this passage is not about clothing, He draws a clear distinction between what a godly man wears and what would be worn in a pagan environment. The Bible draws the same conclusion in Proverbs 7:10 where it says, "…the attire of an harlot." Point being—different types of people dress differently, and clothing certainly identifies us with a lifestyle—a *holy* one or a *lustful* one. To put one point of these verses in plain English: godly men don't dress the same as effeminate men, and godly ladies don't dress like harlots (prostitutes).

Would you consider your dress choices—especially as they pertain to your friendships, your testimony, and who you are becoming? What you wear and how you dress have a powerful impact on your guy/girl relationships. If you dress sleazy and sloppy you are saying, "I don't value myself very much." If you dress to attract attention you are saying, "I'm insecure, and I want to be noticed." We want to challenge you to dress appropriately and modestly for ten basic reasons:

1. To please the Lord Jesus Christ and honor Him above all. So many of our dress decisions are purely based on pleasing self and pleasing others. When you wake up and get dressed, for whom are you dressing? First Corinthians 10:31 teaches, "Whether therefore ye eat, or drink, or whatsoever ye do, do all to the glory of God."

2. To submit to the biblical principle of modesty. This is more of an issue with ladies because men are "sight oriented." If you have a home with only girls, you may not really get this! What some ladies think is "cute" is very often provocative. Dads should be the authority in this area, and moms should work to educate themselves on what their daughters "look like" through the eyes of young men. First Timothy 2:9 teaches, "In like manner also, that women adorn themselves in modest apparel...."

3. To submit to the biblical principle of appropriateness and to identify with godliness. Philippians 4:5 teaches, "Let your moderation be known unto all men. The Lord is at hand." The definition of *moderation* is "appropriateness." While young men might not struggle so much with modesty, they certainly should be taught what is appropriate dress for various environments.

Many young adults act as if wearing their "ballgame" clothing to church is appropriate. It simply isn't. When it comes to dress, we should have a higher respect for spiritual environments than we do for mowing the lawn. It's the same reason we dress better for weddings and funerals—because we respect the people and the environment involved. Why should God get less respect than the dead?

4. To promote an environment of purity and spiritual growth. Sadly, your generation is more sexually educated, active, and tempted than EVER before in American history! With our friends we should be committed to maintaining a pure and godly atmosphere—and that means dress should be modest and appropriate. The way we dress absolutely contributes to our environment and attitudes, and they should be godly and Christ-honoring.

Additionally, we often draw our identity from our clothing! Your generation is highly self-conscious and image-conscious. But you won't grow spiritually if you are consumed with social status and fashion trends.

Think of this "environment principle" like this: What if you needed open heart surgery and the surgeon showed up for surgery wearing flip-flops, cut-off shorts, a tank top, a ball cap, sunglasses, and smelling like sunscreen? You would deem him inappropriate and unfit for surgery!

When my (Cary) daughter was born she was eight weeks early, and for two weeks she had to be kept in the NICU ward of the hospital. Strangely, every time I wanted to hold her or see her, I had to scrub my hands and arms and cover myself in the most odd-looking blue outfit you have ever seen. Why? Because the NICU is a delicate health environment where little lives are at stake. The value of those lives places a premium on the cleanliness of the environment.

> You won't grow spiritually if you are consumed with social status and fashion trends.

The point—how you dress contributes to your environments with friends, at school, and at church.

5. To honor the convictions of our parents or pastor. What could possibly be wrong with simply preferring another person—especially one in spiritual

Twenty-Two—Dress for Success

authority? The Bible is clear on this principle in two ways. First, we are commanded to honor those who have the rule over us. Hebrews 13:17, "Obey them that have the rule over you, and submit yourselves: for they watch for your souls...." Second, we are commanded to prefer one another! Romans 12:10, "Be kindly affectioned one to another with brotherly love; in honour preferring one another."

For younger people, the question of dress is as simple as, "What do my parents want me to wear?" Not "What can I talk or argue them into?"

The attitude that says, "I'll wear what I want no matter what anybody says" is not only rebellious, it is just purely selfish and childish. Any two-year-old can display that on cue! If I know an authority figure prefers that I dress a certain way, I'm right to honor and to prefer my authority just to show love and respect.

Question: Why will we do this for employers, restaurants, golf courses, and bowling alleys (to be explained later), but we won't do it for the Lord? When I (Cary) was sixteen working at McDonald's, they made me wear a blue hat! I didn't like it. I didn't want to wear it. I thought it was stupid. But I wore it—and with a good attitude. Why? Because authority expected it.

6. **To give an account to the Lord with joy.** This one is really big! We really do have to stand before God to answer for what we wear and the thoughts we influence in the minds of others. Second Corinthians 5:10, "For we must all appear before the judgment seat of Christ;

that every one may receive the things done in his body, according to that he hath done, whether it be good or bad."

7. To promote a spirit of maturity. Maturity isn't an age, it is the acceptance of responsibility. And no responsible adult gets to dress the way they want all the time.

The sooner you overcome your fashion-conscious insecurities, the more mature and responsible you will become. First Corinthians 13:11, "When I was a child, I spake as a child, I understood as a child, I thought as a child: but when I became a man, I put away childish things."

God commands you to be an example in 1 Timothy 4:12, "Let no man despise thy youth; but be thou an example of the believers, in word, in conversation, in charity, in spirit, in faith, in purity."

8. To exemplify a distinct lifestyle not conformed to the world. Simply put, the attitude that says, "I can wear what I want when I want and nobody can tell me different" does not reflect a spiritual life but a carnal life. This is a life conformed, not transformed. Ephesians 5:8, "For ye were sometimes darkness, but now are ye light in the Lord: walk as children of light." Romans 12:2, "And be not conformed to this world: but be ye transformed by the renewing of your mind, that ye may prove what is that good, and acceptable, and perfect, will of God."

Twenty-Two—Dress for Success

I still believe that God intends for us to walk "out of step" with the world. This simply isn't the case for modern Christendom. Most Christians are trying to blend in as best as they can with the world's styles. Why do we care what the world thinks more than what the Lord desires? God instructs us in Galatians that even as we are *in* Christ, we are also to *put on* Christ. Most Christians are more than happy to *be in* Christ, but few really desire to *put on* Christ.

9. To protect the thoughts and innocence of peers. You will most likely see more inappropriate clothing by accident during your youth than your grandfather could have looked for in a lifetime.

Choose the safe path! When you dress modestly and appropriately you are saying that you value yourself as God does. You are broadcasting your commitment to purity. You are saying to others, "Think purely about me!" You are protecting their hearts and minds and displaying responsibility and respect.

10. To be a clear witness of the Gospel. Christians who dress appropriately are delightfully different! They shine brightly for Christ in a carnal culture.

Not long ago, I (Cary) had a large group of senior-highers at an In-N-Out Burger (a Southern California fast-food favorite). The group was dressed sharp; they acted respectfully; and they were kind to others in the restaurant. (For instance, our teens allow other people to take the front of the line whenever our entire group is in line at a restaurant.) Toward the end of our visit, two adults approached me and asked where these "wonderful students" were from. I happily said, "Lancaster Baptist Church"—to which they replied, "Well, this sure gives us hope for the next generation! What a great group of young people!"

I was so thankful for the testimony that the Lord allowed us to have at that moment. Why can't we remember that man always looks on the outward appearance (1 Samuel 16:7)? Jesus taught us in Matthew 5:16, "Let your light so shine before men, that they may see your good works, and glorify your Father which is in heaven."

Everybody knows that dress matters. It's really just a matter of submitting our selfish wills to God and living to please Him first.

These same principles would apply to hairstyles, makeup, manners and other areas of outward conduct as well. Perhaps as you read these principles you thought, "Well, that's just not *me*. I have to be *me*." May I gently encourage you to give up that self-centered thought process. I figured out a long time ago that "having to be me" in these types of areas was a losing proposition—and a very limiting one. The winning life is really about surrendering your identity fully to Jesus Christ.

Just trust the Lord and His Word. Set aside your own preferences or self-centered thinking. Decide to dress in a way that absolutely pleases the Lord and shows respect for Him in every environment.

Twenty-Two—Dress for Success

In closing, let us contextualize these thoughts. Encouraging you to dress to honor the Lord is not about legalism or arrogance. We shouldn't be "Gestapo" about this. We shouldn't look down on someone who doesn't dress perfectly to our standard. We should be compassionate towards them.

As you raise your personal standards in this area, please do so with tenderness and compassion towards others. Decent dress doesn't produce a right heart—it should reflect one! Christ-honoring dress should be the product of a pure heart, not the white-washed exterior of a proud one.

Finally, we have not tried to define your standards in this chapter. That's up to your parents or authorities, the Lord, and His Word.

> The winning life is really about surrendering your identity fully to Jesus Christ.

If your standard isn't ours, we are not accountable for that. Our standard doesn't define spirituality, it merely defines what God has put on our hearts for our families and ministries. It defines how we best apply the principles of God's Word. You must define your standard by your authorities and God's principles, and be prepared to answer to Him for it. One final story and we're done.

Not long ago I (Cary) was with my family strolling through an open shopping area when we happened upon a new bowling alley that served lunch to your lane. We needed lunch, and bowling sounded fun, so a few moments later, we were bowling, eating, and making some great memories. It wasn't until we were leaving that I noticed a large sign at the entrance explaining the dress code. I read this sign in disbelief.

The rules were as follows: *No sweatshirts or sports jerseys, no jogging pants or jumpsuits, no MC colors, no hats or headgear, no baggy clothing, all clothing must be neat and clean, no long shorts, no boots, no long or baggy T-shirts, no sleeveless shirts, and no solid color T-shirts.* Wow! All that just for bowling!

In closing, think about that bowling alley. Somebody there really respects that environment. When it comes to dress—do you care as much about honoring the Lord as they do about bowling?

Your appearance—your dress choices—will contribute much to your friendships. If you dress in a way that honors the Lord, your friendships will benefit too.

TWENTY-THREE
What to Do When You Can't Act Normal

When you're with a guy or girl, building a Christ-centered, healthy friendship, what do you talk about? Let's face it, the younger years make for some awkward social moments between guys and girls. It's easy for your emotions to get tweaked and make you feel weird and socially dysfunctional.

Just recently I (Cary) was having a conversation with a teenage young man about relating with girls. His question—"How am I supposed to act?" My answer—"Just act normal." At this point, he began to laugh hysterically, repeating my answer over and over—like I had said, "Grow another head." You would have thought that "acting normal" was an absolute impossibility—and indeed it sometimes is when young emotions are at play.

I tried again by saying, "Just be yourself"—which also got a good round of laughter. Then I just gave up.

We still believe you should be able to be yourself! But since in some young minds it is apparently *impossible* to act normal or be yourself, we would like to complete this chapter with some suggestions of how to communicate—what to talk about—as you act "abnormal" and attempt to "be someone other than yourself."

What God Says about Communication

"But let your communication be, Yea, yea; Nay, nay: for whatsoever is more than these cometh of evil" (Matthew 5:37).

"Let no corrupt communication proceed out of your mouth, but that which is good to the use of edifying, that it may minister grace unto the hearers" (Ephesians 4:29).

"Notwithstanding ye have well done, that ye did communicate with my affliction" (Philippians 4:14).

"Be not deceived: evil communications corrupt good manners" (1 Corinthians 15:33).

The most important thing you do with friends is talk. Words are powerful, and God commands you to use your words to strengthen and edify. He commands you to put away all filthy or corrupt communication and to embrace pure words that build.

Twenty-Three—When You Can't Act Normal

What a blessing for God to give us words to tell others of our feelings, thoughts, opinions, and love. Words can be used to help or hurt, to love or hate, for good or evil, and even for winning people to Christ. Since communication is one of the foundations of marriage, it is essential for successful friendships.

Learning to Communicate

You will be a happier person if you can learn proper conversational skills. You will feel more comfortable around others. God will use you as an instrument for Him. Remember Moses? He thought that he could not speak well, but God changed that and he became one of the best leaders Israel ever had.

One of the best reasons to keep your friendship "group oriented" is because there are more people to talk to and more things to talk about. Your communication becomes more open and others-focused. This is healthy for a good friendship.

Earlier in the book we talked about laughter, and as long as you're laughing at wholesome things, laughter between friends is also a great avenue of communication. Everybody likes to laugh.

Here are some suggestions how to communicate well as you grow in friendship:

1. Talk about each other's interests. Don't do all the talking yourself. Learn about others by asking questions and listening. Share your testimony of salvation, your future plans, your interests, your hobbies, and your life experiences with each other. Discover what you have in common.

2. **Give your full attention.** Don't look off in the distance, at your watch, or some other distraction. Be attentive to every word.

3. **Be complimentary but not excessively.** Everyone likes to be complimented and spoken to with encouraging and uplifting words.

4. **Be willing to laugh at yourself.** Sometimes we take ourselves too seriously. Keep things light.

5. **Talk about Christ-honoring things.** Never talk about questionable subjects. Philippians 4:8, "Finally, brethren, whatsoever things are true, whatsoever things are honest, whatsoever things are just, whatsoever things are pure, whatsoever things are lovely, whatsoever things are of good report; if there be any virtue, and if there be any praise, think on these things." Anything that fits this criteria is acceptable to talk about with a friend.

6. **Talk about blessings you have recently received.**

7. **Talk about Bible truths you have recently learned.** Share verses and truths you've learned in your walk with God. Share decisions you've made for the Lord.

8. **Talk about answers to prayer or prayer requests.** Share what God has done or what you are asking Him to do.

Twenty-Three—When You Can't Act Normal

9. Share soulwinning experiences. Christian young people ought to be able to encourage each other in sharing their faith with others.

10. As impossible as it might seem, try to be yourself. It's okay to feel awkward—you're young and growing. Awkwardness is a part of the territory. Just ask God to help you be who He made you to be. You're one of a kind, and others will find you most interesting when you are just yourself!

In your future, you will spend more time *communicating* in your marriage than doing anything else. It won't matter if you can kiss well or hold hands like a pro. If you can't relate—talk, carry on a conversation—your marriage will be in bad shape!

You can't kiss for twenty-four hours a day—but you will be married twenty-four hours a day. Let's just be generous and say you're going to kiss an hour a day after you're married—which is highly unlikely. What are you going to do with the other twenty-three hours a day for the rest of your life?

You'd better learn how to be great friends—and great friends know how to talk.

Think About It
Chapters 21–23

Assignment for Personal Application

Find a quiet place, a blank paper, and think through these practical exercises. Consider sharing this exercise with a parent, friend, a group of friends, or a teacher.

1. List the etiquette rules that you most need to work on in your life.

2. Which principle of dress and appearance most challenged you? Why?

3. Think about the last conversation you had with your friend. Describe what it was about. Did the subject edify you both or not?

4. List five spiritually edifying topics or questions you will talk through with your friend soon.

5. Write one or two paragraphs describing what God did in your heart through this book.

Memorize these verses: "Whether therefore ye eat, or drink, or whatsoever ye do, do all to the glory of God" (1 Corinthians 10:31).

"Let no corrupt communication proceed out of your mouth, but that which is good to the use of edifying, that it may minister grace unto the hearers" (Ephesians 4:29).

Conclusion

Well, here we are at the end of this book, and we still don't know what to call this thing between guys and girls. It's real. It's here to stay. It's normal. It's even wonderful.

It's also dangerous. It's deceptive. It's strange and tricky. It's delightful and confusing at the same time. It's scary for authorities and intriguing for young adults. It teases the heart and heightens the senses.

It is new. You haven't been here for very long. You like it, but it's also awkward, and you feel a little clumsy about it. It's embarrassing. But it's also promising. It's pleasing but also overwhelming.

Part of you wants to follow it with all of your heart, and part of you wants to run back to third grade and never return. Part of you doesn't want to talk about it, and part of you wants to talk of nothing else!

You want to be liked. You like being liked. You hope someone will like you. You would like someone to *like*. But liking and being liked is risky business. It puts your heart into someone else's hands and theirs into yours. They could hurt it. You could hurt theirs. They could take advantage of it. They could break it. Your heart doesn't belong in their hands. Neither does theirs in yours. The heart belongs only in God's hands.

There are great lessons to be learned. There are great risks to be avoided. This journey through young adult emotions and attractions can be survived. It can be navigated wisely. You must make it! You can't afford to be a casualty. You can't afford to lose your heart, your purity, or your sanity. You must make it to that wonderful someday.

Thank you for reading. In these pages we have given you the tools, the knowledge, and the biblical principles you need to survive. As we pen these final words, our hearts go out to you with passionate prayers for your safe arrival into the someday of marriage and family life. We are grateful that you have given us the time and influence. You have opened your heart and allowed us to place within it the right values, the right thinking, and the right choices from God's Word.

Now it's time to respond. Erase Hollywood's model and embrace God's. Through your young adult years, we urge you to keep things light. Have godly friendships

Conclusion

that strengthen your life. Keep your heart safely in God's hands. Keep your purity gift-wrapped and waiting for a spouse. Keep your emotions controlled by the Spirit of your loving Heavenly Father. Keep your behavior appropriate and your hands to yourself. Keep your words wholesome and your communications Christ-honoring. Keep your relationships healthy and balanced. And above all, keep your God first and foremost!

Somewhere in the soon-coming will of God, there is most likely waiting a very special relationship. When God intersects your life with the right person at the right time, all the wonderful desires of your heart will be fulfilled by God's good grace.

Then it will be the right time to stop being *just friends…*

For then, you will be *more than friends.*

And that's a different book entirely…

To be continued…

My flesh and my heart faileth: but God is the strength of my heart, and my portion for ever. —PSALM 73:26

Just Friends in Review

The Big Principles
» Youth is filled with big transitions—emotional, physical, and mental.
» Friendships should be for fellowship and spiritual growth.
» Hollywood's Model—*finding the "right person"* always fails.
» God's Model—*becoming the right person* always works.
» God is preparing you for a wonderful someday—sow the right seeds.

The Eight Choices of a Healthy Guy/Girl Friendship
» Choose "the right person at the right time."

- » Choose to stay in god's will.
- » Choose Holy Spirit controlled emotions.
- » Choose to stay pure until marriage.
- » Choose not to touch each other.
- » Choose to keep family first.
- » Choose true love over lust.
- » Choose the "just friends" approach.

The Practical Tools for a Healthy Relationship

- » Work on becoming a person with quality character traits.
- » Make commitments and ask for help in setting the right pace.
- » Consider the many advantages of not being obligated.
- » Learn the basics of appropriate etiquette.
- » Make sure you dress in a way that pleases God and protects others.
- » Practice communication skills—the most needed marriage skill.

Visit us online

strivingtogether.com

dailyintheword.org

wcbc.edu

lancasterbaptist.org

paulchappell.com

Also available from **Cary Schmidt**

Discover Your Destiny
In these pages, you will be guided step by step through the biblical principles that will help you discover God's plan for your life. You will gain the tools you need to make right choices. You will delight in God's guiding principles for decision-making and equip yourself to discover your destiny! (280 pages, paperback)

Life Quest
Life Quest is a guide to braving adulthood with biblical passion. This book will place you on a forward path of biblical principles. Don't waste another day in what some call a "perpetual state of limbo"! Discover the true rewards of living God's purpose and embracing the challenges of adulthood! (272 pages, hardback)

Different by Design
This personal Bible study reveals God's heart for a biblical lifestyle. You will be challenged not to separate "who you are" from "how you behave." You will be reminded that a godly life is a different life and that God's way of living is still the best way! (240 pages, paperback)

strivingtogether.com

Also available from
Striving Together Publications

The Spiritual Leader
The Spiritual Leader summarizes a biblical philosophy of spiritual leadership that has been lived out dynamically through the life of the author. Every principle in these chapters flows from the Word of God and from a heart that has effectively served God's people for over twenty-five years. (336 pages, hardback)

What's on Your Mind?
This book is about letting the mind of the Master become the master of your mind! It is about bringing more than human willpower to bear in controlling and reigning in the power of your thoughts. It is about true, lasting, and biblical life-change. Each page applies God's truth to the battle that every Christian fights every day—the battle of the mind. (184 pages, paperback)

It's a Wonderful Life
From the very first page, your heart will be uplifted by Terrie's candid, humorous, and down-to-earth approach to loving God, supporting your husband, and serving God's people both biblically and joyfully. Discover that it really is a "wonderful life" when your life is dedicated to Jesus Christ! (280 pages, hardback)

strivingtogether.com